THE AWESOME EXPERIMENTS

Learning the language of chemistry through experiments for Children and More

By

Steve Huxley

Table of Contents

INTRODUCTION

You are one of the very luckiest of people-to be growing up in the Age of Science. For a long while, boys and girls used to say, "I wish I were a pioneer," or "I wish there were something left to discover." Nowadays, it is clear that science offers a great variety of new things to discover and that many of the new pioneers will be scientists.

Physical science is the study of matter and energy. Chemistry is one of the physical sciences.' It teaches us much about the different kinds of matter and how they behave. It teaches how different chemicals react with each other so that you can tell in advance what will happen when you mix certain chemicals. This knowledge has helped chemists decide what fuels to use to propel rockets and push satellites into space. But you cannot work with nuclear reactors or rocket fuels until you first learn the fundamental facts of chemistry.

This book will help you to do just that.

Remember that you didn't learn to roller-skate, or to ride a bicycle, until you could balance yourself on your feet. You cannot devise new chemical reactions until you can balance chemical equations. It's fun to mix things in a laboratory and to guess or predict the results. You may not always be correct in your predictions, nor will you always be correct in your mixing, but it will always be fun to account for every single atom involved in a chemical reaction. You will learn how to do this gradually, as you do the experiments in this book.

You must remember to follow the safety rules, to be neat and careful, to avoid contaminating your chemicals, and to be especially conscientious about reporting observations accurately. A true scientist would never put away a dirty test tube or falsify a report.

In this book, you will learn the language of chemistry and find that it is not a bit mysterious, but simple and interesting to use. And when you read science articles in newspapers and magazines you will surprise yourself by understanding them so well. If you enjoy this work and do it well, you will probably continue it; then maybe someday you will make a great discovery that will broaden the horizons of science.

Before doing any experiment in this book, you should always read the instructions for that experiment. Then you will know before you begin what equipment and chemicals you will need, and you will have an idea in advance of the procedures you are supposed to follow. There will undoubtedly be chemicals that you have never heard of mentioned in the experiments. Look them up in the chart, and you will find that many are ordinary household substances that you or your parents use nearly every day.

It is up to you to decide whether you want to read the section entitled"Results" before or after experimenting. Of course, there would be more suspense if you wait until afterward to read it and see if you have observed what it says, but the choice depends on your work habits.

Much exciting knowledge awaits you as you prepare to explore the world of chemistry.

NOTE: experiments marked with an asterisk (*) are potentially dangerous. Parents should decide how much supervision is necessary.

THE LANGUAGE OF CHEMISTRY

By the time you are old enough to read this book, you will surely have heard people using words like these: atom, molecule, element, and compound. You may know what some of them mean, but others may seem too difficult to worry about. You may have seen some strange combinations of numbers and letters, too, like those shown here, and wondered what in the world they could mean:

$$2NaHCO_3 + H_2So_4 \text{-+} 2Co_2 + 2H_2O + Na_2SO_4$$

This is the language of chemistry. Before you begin to learn this language, there is one very important thing to know. All of science is based on laws of nature, and the laws of nature are simple and dependable. If you let go of a rock you are holding, it will fall to the ground. If water gets cold enough, it will freeze. If you add 2 and 2 correctly, you will always get 4. The sun always rises in the east and sets in the west. These are laws of nature; we can depend upon them. Could anything be more simple or more satisfying?

Chemistry, like all the physical sciences, is based on the laws of nature too.

When the same *atoms* (the smallest whole particles of matter) or combinations of atoms come together under the same circumstances, the same chemical reactions always take place. Time after time, chemists have found molecules (small groups of atoms bound together chemically) behaving in the same way, when conditions governing them are the same.

Now let's try to understand this language of the chemist. Atoms and molecules are not always synonymous, but in certain cases they are. An atom, by itself, is a single unit, so an atom cannot be made any simpler, except under exceptional circumstances. A molecule may consist of one atom or more than one. Thus it can often be made simpler.

Chemists have agreed on a sort of scientific shorthand in which letters stand for the names of *elements*, substances composed of only one kind of atom.

They call these letters chemical symbols. Combinations of symbols represent the different atoms in a particular kind of molecule. These combinations are called *formulas*, and they show what elements are contained in a *compound*.

A compound, as you can probably tell, is a substance made up of molecules containing atoms of more than one element. The way a chemist uses numbers in this scientific shorthand shows the proportion of different kinds of atoms in the molecules of a compound. By agreeing to use the same system of symbols and formulas, the chemists have made it possible for every scientist to understand any chemical reaction written in the language of chemistry. Even when scientists of different countries speak different languages, the language of chemistry remains the same and understandable to everyone.

Now, using the atoms of the common elements, let's look at how this language works. You will see that it is really simple.

Ag is the symbol for the element silver. *Cl* is the symbol for the element chlorine. When made to react with each other, a silver atom and a chlorine atom combine to become a molecule of silver chloride, or *AgCl*. Here is how this reaction looks when stated in the language of chemistry:

$$Ag + Cl \longrightarrow AgCl$$

This formula states that one atom of silver and one atom of chlorine become, or, to use a more technical term, yield one molecule of silver chloride. The statement itself is in the form of an *equation*. No numbers are used when an "I" would be the appropriate number; the "I" is understood. But this does not necessarily mean that only one atom of silver and one atom of chlorine were involved. Perhaps the reaction involved several million atoms of each kind.

Atoms are so tiny that it probably involved many more than that. What the understood "I" does mean is that for every one atom of silver that joined one atom of chlorine, *one* molecule of silver chloride was formed.

Na is the symbol for sodium. See if you can explain what this equation means:

$$Na + Cl \longrightarrow NaCI$$

Whenever two or more atoms remain bound together, they make up a molecule. For molecules to be of the same kind, the atoms they contain must be present in the same relative numbers. This consistent grouping of the same number combinations in one kind of substance is called the Law of Definite Proportions. You are surely familiar with the formula for a molecule of water, H_2O. It doesn't look like AgCl or NaCl. It has a 2 in it, and the 2 is written as a small subscript (something written below the line). This formula says that one molecule of water contains two atoms of hydrogen (the H) and one atom of oxygen (the O). Whenever two atoms of hydrogen unite with one atom of oxygen, the result is one molecule of water. This is one of the basic laws in chemistry. How would you explain this formula: H_2O_2? It represents one molecule, of course, but not of water. In water the *ratio* (the relative proportion) is 2 to 1; in this molecule, the ratio is 2 to 2. Therefore it can't be water. It'shydrogen peroxide (the same peroxide you use on cuts). When the ratio of different kinds of atoms in a molecule changes, the substance becomes completely different.

If H is the symbol for hydrogen, then what does H_2 mean? H is one atom of hydrogen alone, but the 2 in H_2 means there are two atoms of hydrogen, so H_2 must be a molecule. H_2 is one molecule of hydrogen which contains two atoms of the same kind, that is, hydrogen. Can this be true of O_2 too?

Yes, one molecule of oxygen contains two oxygen atoms.

Now if the small numbers in the subscript represent the number of atoms in one molecule, what do the big numbers written on the same line mean? Look at this equation:

$$2H_2 + O_2 \longrightarrow 2H_2O$$

The big 2 in front of H_2 shows that there are two hydrogen molecules. Each of these molecules contains two atoms of hydrogen. The subscript 2 says so.

Then how many atoms of hydrogen are represented here? Four. Having two molecules of two atoms each is like having two bags each containing two apples.

All together you'd have four apples. The big 2 in front of the formula for water means that there are also two molecules of water. But in each of these molecules, there are three atoms, two of hydrogen and one of oxygen. If there are three atoms in one molecule, then there are six atoms in two molecules. But remember that the mathematical proportions are always the same in molecules of the same substance. In these two water molecules, there are four atoms of hydrogen and two atoms of oxygen. This is like having two bags, each containing two apples and one lemon, or a total of four apples and two lemons.

Why are these large numbers necessary? Because of another of the basic laws of nature, the one that says: Matter cannot be created or destroyed; only its form can be changed. This is the Law of Conservation of Matter. If you wrote:

$$H_2 + O_2 \rightarrow H_2O$$

you would be describing an impossible reaction.

You would be throwing away one atom of oxygen, something that not even the greatest scientists in the world can do. For an equation to tell the truth and account for all the atoms, both sides of it must be balanced. One of the things you must do then to correct a wrong equation is to balance it by changing the numbers. You can't change the subscript numbers, though, because the Law of Definite Proportions says the ratio of different atoms in one kind of molecule must remain the same. You can't throw in new atoms or throw out old ones either because the Law of Conservation of Matter says that matter cannot be created or destroyed. The only numbers you can change, then, to balance an equation are the numbers of molecules. Instead of saying $H_2 + O_2 \longrightarrow H_2O$, you must say:

$$2H_2 + O_2 \longrightarrow 2H_2O$$

This is the same as saying: 4(H's) + 2(o's) 4(H's) + 2(o's). In regular language, the equation now says: when four atoms of hydrogen unite with two atoms of oxygen, two molecules of water result. Think about this for a while and see if you can explain how and why the equation is now balanced.

As you begin to do your experiments, try to get into the habit of using symbols, formulas, and equations. But never let incorrect ones stay uncorrected.

It would be misleading to you and to anyone who might read your notebook.

An incorrect equation is even worse than a misspelled word.

You have undoubtedly noticed that the' symbols for some of the elements are the same as the first letter or first two letters of the element. Others, such as Na for sodium, are not the same at all. The reason is that the symbols are based on the Latin (or Latinized) names for the elements. In many cases, it just happens that the first letters of the Latin and English names for an element are the same.

Here are some of the most common elements with symbols unlike their first letters:

Element	Latin Name	Symbol
copper	*cuprum*	Cu
gold	*aurum*	Au
iron	*ferrum*	Fe
lead	*plumbum*	Pb
mercury	*hydrargyrum*	Hg
potassium	*kalium*	K
silver	*argentum*	Ag
sodium	*natrium*	Na

There are also certain clues to understanding the verbal language of chemistry. Obviously, when you see the names of certain elements or roots of the names in a compound, you can tell that those elements are contained in the compound. Thus if you see the phrase "sodium chloride," you know that it refers to a compound containing the elements sodium and chlorine. There are also a number of common prefixes and suffixes used in the language of chemistry that tell you about the composition of a compound. The suffix "ide," for example, means simply "in combination with." Sodium chloride then is simply sodium in combination with chlorine. The suffix "ate," however, indicates the presence of oxygen as well. Thus "potassium chlorate" must consist not only of potassium and chlorine but also of oxygen.

Certain atoms group together very tightly in a unit known as a *radical*, which you will learn more about later. For now, all you need to know is that some of the most common radicals are the sulfate radical, consisting of sulfur and oxygen; the nitrate radical, consisting of nitrogen and oxygen; and the hydroxyl radical, consisting of hydrogen and oxygen. Therefore, whenever you see the words sulfate, nitrate, hydroxy, or hydroxyl in a compound, you know that the compound contains these radicals.

There are a number of prefixes that show the number of particular atoms or radicals contained in a compound. Some of the most common are "di" and"bi," meaning 2; "tri," meaning 3; "tetra," meaning 4; and "pent," meaning 5.

Thus, ammonium dichromate indicates the presence of 2 chromate radicals and sodium tetraborate the presence of 4 borate radicals.

Once you have learned these fundamental "clues," you have gone a long way in understanding the language of chemistry.

SETTING UP YOUR LABORATORY

In some ways, a laboratory is very much like a library; but instead of looking up information, the laboratory worker finds out about it for himself. In both places the working conditions are similar. Librarians must catalog books in a library and store them in a neat and orderly fashion. Chemists must label their equipment and chemicals in a laboratory and store them in an equally neat and orderly manner. Silence in a library is essential, so the people using it can concentrate on their work. Silence is essential in a laboratory too, so the workers can give their complete attention to their work. For these reasons, and also for the sake of safety and convenience, you will want to find some special place at home in which to establish your laboratory. It must be reasonably quiet and out of everyone else's way. It must be well lighted and there must be a sink in the laboratory, or very close by, so you can easily get water. To be completely on the safe side, it should be in a place that the younger children can't get to easily. Your fascinating collection of apparatus and chemicals may tempt them to try things that might prove dangerous. Once you have chosen a good location you will need these things:

1. A large table on which to perform your experiments. You should cover it with a heat- or chemical-proof substance, such as linoleum, glass, or tile. If this is not possible, several layers of newspaper, which you must change regularly, will do.

2. Above your work area, there should be one or two shelves on which to keep your chemicals-all, of course, properly labeled and stored, either alphabetically or in groups according to the type of experiment in which you may use them. There is one important exception to this, however. Do not place an acid, such as vinegar, near an *alkali*, such as ammonia. Enough molecules of each substance can escape even from closed bottles to cause a chemical reaction in the surrounding air. The reaction could contaminate the outside of the bottles and the chemicals nearby.

3. Your laboratory apparatus will include those items which you can make yourself, a few which you will have to purchase, plus many things you can collect, such as baby food jars, small plastic bottles and corks of different sizes. Keep all of these in separate places on the shelves or in drawers or boxes which are clearly labeled. '

4. Be sure to have at least one ceramic or pottery waste container for discarded, used, or unwanted solid chemicals, broken glass, and the remains of successful experiments. To get rid of liquid wastes, you must pour them into a sink, with the water constantly running, or put them into a separate metal waste container.

Your laboratory, like your desk, is essentially yours. It should meet your needs and convenience and should suit your methods of working. It is also your responsibility. You must see that the work you do there doesn't cause danger, inconvenience, or worry to anyone else.

EQUIPMENT YOU WILL NEED

Equipment You May Find at Home or Easily Buy

- aluminum foil
- aluminum pie pans
- apron, rubber or plastic
- asbestos pad
- candles, large and small
- cellophane tape
- cigarette lighter
- coffee can
- colorless nail polish
- construction paper, black
- copper wire
- cord or string
- corks
- dishpan
- drawing paper, black and white
- drinking straws
- dry cells, 1 ½ - volt
- eyedropper
- flashlight
- funnels (1 large and I small)
- glass chimneys (2)
- glass jars in ½ pint, pint, quart and gallon sizes
- glass plates, oblong or square
- hammer
- index cards
- ink, black India
- matches
- measuring cup
- nails
- paper and pencil
- paper clips
- paper towels
- paring knife or penknife
- pots and pans
- pyrex bowls, small
- rubber bands
- scale
- scissors steel wool pads, soapless
- teaspoons and tablespoons
- thermometer, weather
- triangular file
- waste containers, ceramic and metal
- wrapping paper

Equipment You Can Buy from a Chemical Supply House

(You can buy this equipment directly or order it by mail from any chemical supply house listed in the yellow pages of your telephone book. Look for the one nearest to your home.)

- alcohol burner
- beaker
- filter paper
- flame spreader
- flasks (2)
- glass rod (one 3-foot length)
- glass tubing (one 4- or 6-foot length)
- litmus paper, red and blue
- rubber stoppers (three l-holed and three 2-holed)
- rubber tubing to fit glass tubing (one 4- or 6-foot length) test tube, pyrex
- test tubes, glass (24)
- thistle tubes (2)
- wood splints (l small package)

You won't need a great deal of expensive laboratory apparatus to perform the experiments in this book. You can make much of the equipment yourself from ordinary things you will find at home. Don't be afraid to invent things of your own. Many scientists are constantly devising new pieces of equipment because there is nothing suitable in their laboratories for the new experiments they think up.

How to Make a Test Tube Holder

Cut a 12-inch piece of wire from the lower edge of a wire coat hanger. Use a wire cutter or a pair of wire-cutting pliers. Or, with an ordinary pair of blunt-tipped pliers, bend the wire back and forth until it breaks. Starting at one end, wrap the wire around a dowel stick of about the same diameter as your test tubes. Start wrapping the wire from the top of the dowel stick and make at least three turns downward. Remove the dowel and bend the other end of the wire into a loop to use as a handle. Try the wire holder around one test tube for size. The tube should fit within the coils loosely, but shouldn't slide through. The edge of the tube should rest on the uppermost coil. If the tube doesn't fit correctly into the holder, adjust the coils until it does. You might want to make several test tube holders.

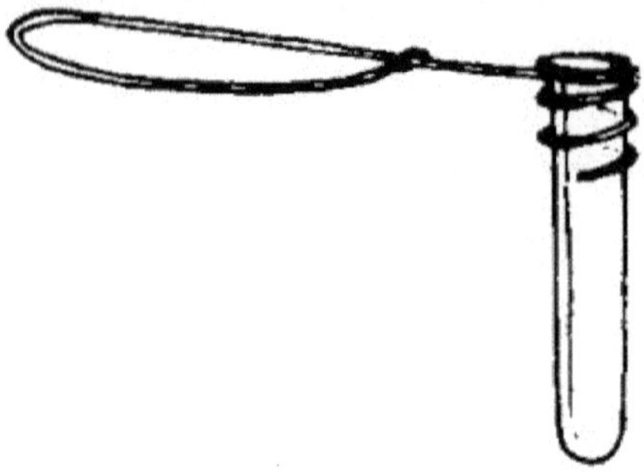

How to Make a Test Tube Rack

Find an empty but sturdy shoebox that is not quite as wide as your test tubes are long. Remove the cover and stand the box on its side, with the open part facing you. Using the top edge of a test tube as a guide, trace six circles in a straight line on the uppermost side. Now cut them out with a pair of scissors or your penknife. Cut the rim off the cover, and fit the cover into the box parallel to the sides. If it's too large to fit into the box, trim it where necessary. Stick a pencil down through the holes in the side of the box to the trimmed-off cover, and make marks on it, directly below the center of each hole. Now cut out holes around these marks and make them the same size as the other six holes.

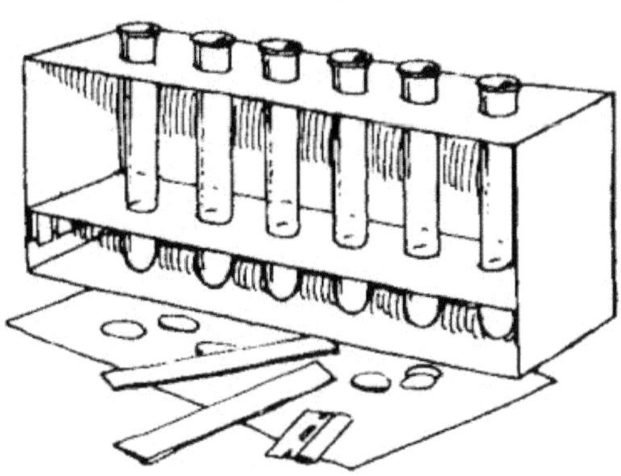

The side of the box will be the rack as you have probably guessed and the trimmed-off cover will be a shelf underneath it. With cellophane tape attach the shelf to the walls of the rack about 1 inch from the bottom. Slip an empty test tube into each hole in the top and through the hole directly below it. If you traced the holes correctly, the tubes will fit. Cover the surfaces of your test tube rack with aluminum foil to make it last longer. You will need several of these racks, and you will want to replace them as soon as they become wet or contaminated with chemicals. If you have test tubes of more than one size, you will have to find different boxes to fit the various sizes.

How to Make a Wire Gauze Pad

From aluminum screening (the kind used in summer window screens) cut a 5-inch square. With a dark pencil or a piece of chalk, measure! of an inch in from each side and draw a square. Measure! an inch in from each side of the square you just drew, and draw a second square. Now, using a metal or metal-edged ruler as a guide, fold in the screening in the outside square. Do this on all four sides. After making the first fold, and still using the ruler as a guide, fold in on the second line. You may find it difficult to manage the corners. If so, tap them gently with a hammer.

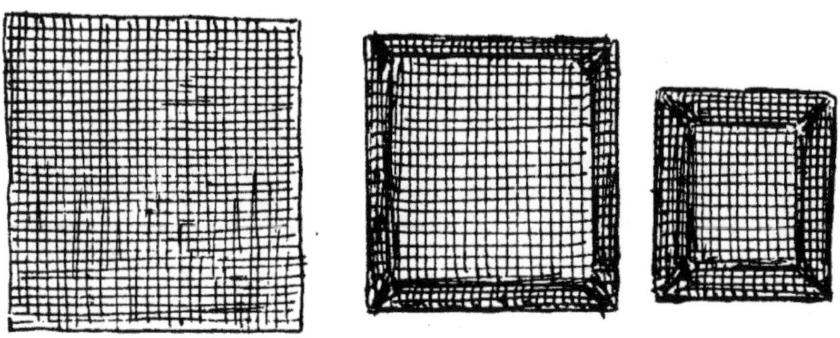

Now you have a wire gauze pad that can withstand the heat of your alcohol burner, and which will not endanger your fingers while you are using it. To use it, you place it over the ring support and rest on it in the container you wish to heat. You will probably want several wire gauze pads.

How to Make a Ring Support and a Clamp-on and Upright Stand

For the stand, obtain a piece of wood 6 inches long, 4 inches wide, and ½ inch thick. Find the center by drawing diagonal lines from opposite corners. Drill a ⅜ inch hole through the board at the central point. Get a dowel stick i of an inch in diameter and 2 feet in length. With the help of the shop teacher in your school or your father at home, drill alternate ¼ inch and ⅛ inch holes in the dowel stick at intervals of 2 inches, beginning 4 inches from one end. You will be able to use these holes to hold either the ring support or the clamp. Insert the dowel stick into the hole in the center of the board.

To make the ring support, cut a 10-inch length of coat hanger wire. Measure 6 inches from one end. With a pair of blunt-end pliers, bend the wire at this point to form one loop or circle. This loop will support a funnel, a crucible, an evaporating dish, a wire gauze pad, or other pieces of apparatus. To use the ring support, insert the straight end of it into one of the small holes in the upright dowel stick, at the desired height.

To make the clamp, obtain a ¼ inch dowel stick, 6 inches long. Glue one end of the "handle" of a pinch-type clothespin to the end of the dowel stick, and for extra strength wrap the two together with fine steel wire, pulled tight and twisted with the blunt-end pliers. When you squeeze it to an "open" position, the clothespin will hold a test tube, glass tubing, or other pieces of equipment. As with the ring support, you can insert this clamp into any suitable hole in the upright dowel that is at the correct height for your needs.

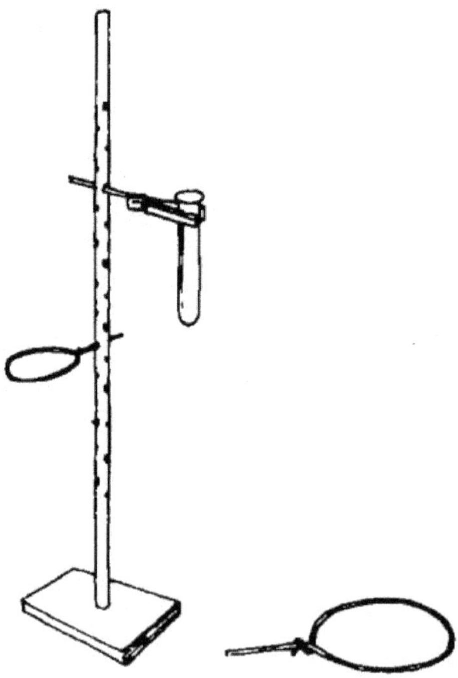

CHEMICALS YOU WILL NEED

Chemical Name	***Formula***	***Common Name***	***Where Available***
Acetic acid	CH3COOH	vinegar	grocery store
Acetone	CH3COCH3	nail polish remover	drugstore
Acetylsalicylic acid	CH3COOC$_6$H4COOH	aspirin	drugstore
Ammonium dichromate	(NH4)2Cr2O7		chemical supply house
Ammonium hydroxide	NH4OH	ammonia water	grocery store
Benzene	C_6H_6	benzol	drugstore
Boracic acid	H3BO3	boric acid	drugstore
Calcium bicarbonate	Ca(HCO3)2		drugstore
Calcium carbonate	CaCO3	chalk	stationery store
Calcium chloride hypochlorite	CaOCI2	chloride of lime	drugstore
Calcium hydroxide	Ca(OH)2	slaked lime	drugstore
Calcium oxide	CaO		chemical supply house
Calcium sulfate	CaSO4	gypsum	drugstore
Carbon	C	basic ingredient of coal	coal dealer
Carbon tetrachloride	CCI4	ingredient of solvents and	grocery store

		detergents	
Carbonic acid	H_2CO_3	soda water	grocery store
Cobalt chloride	$CoCl_2$		chemical supply house
Copper ammonium sulfate	$CuSO_4NH_4OH$	Benedict's solution	drugstore
Copper sulfate	$CuSO_4$	blue vitriol	drugstore
Ethanol	C_2H_5OH	grain alcohol	drugstore
Ferric ammonium sulfate	$Fe_2(SO_4)_3(NH_4)_2SO_4$	ingredients of old-fashioned ink	stationery store
Sodium ferrocyanide	$Na_4Fe(CN)_6$	ingredients of old-fashioned ink	stationery store
Ferric oxalate	$Fe_2(C_2O_4)_3$		drugstore
Ferrous sulfate	$FeSO_4$	green vitriol	chemical supply house
Glucose	$C_6H_{12}O_6$	Dextrose corn syrup	drugstore
Glycerol	$C_3H_5(OH)_3$	glycerine	drugstore
Hydrogen peroxide	H_2O_2	peroxide	drugstore
Hydroquinone	$C_6H_4(OH)_2$		drugstore
Hypochlorous acid	HCIO	laundry bleach	grocery store
Iodine, tincture of	I in alcohol solution	iodine	drugstore
Lead nitrate	$Pb(NO_3)_2$		chemical supply house
Magnesium (ribbon)	Mg		chemical supply house

Magnesium sulfate	MgSO4	Epsom salts	drugstore
Manganese dioxide	MnO2		chemical supply house
Manganous sulfate	MnSO4		chemical supply house
Mercurous chloride	HgCI	calomel	chemical supply house
Mercury	Hg	quicksilver	chemical supply house
Methanol	CH3OH	wood alcohol (	chemical supply house
Naphthalene	C10H8	mothballs	hardware store
Nitric acid	HNO3		chemical supply house
Octane	C8H18	ingredient of gasoline	gasoline station
Paraformaldehyde	CH2O2		drugstore
Potassium aluminum sulfate	AI2(SO4)3K2SO4	alum	drugstore
Potassium carbonate	K2CO3	washing soda	grocery store
Potassium ferricyanide	K3Fe(CN)6		chemical supply house
Potassium hydrotartrate	KH(C4H4O6)	cream of tartar	grocery store
Potassium permanganate	KMnO4		drugstore
Pyrogallic acid	C6H3(OH)3		drugstore
Silicon dioxide	SiO2	sand	chemical supply house

Silver nitrate	$AgNO_3$		drugstore
Sodium bicarbonate	$NaHCO_3$	baking soda	grocery store
Sodium carbonate	Na_2CO_3	soda ash	drugstore
Sodium chloride	NaCI	salt	grocery store
Sodium hydroxide	NaOH	caustic soda	grocery store
Sodium nitrate	$NaNO_3$	saltpeter	chemical supply house
Sodium silicate	Na_2SiO_3		drugstore
Sodium tetraborate	$Na_2B_4O_7$	borax	grocery store
Sodium thiosulfate	$Na_2S_2O_3$	hypo	drugstore
Starch	$C_6H_{10}O_5$	laundry starch	grocery store
Stearic acid	$C_{17}H_{35}COOH$	ingredient of tallow	grocery store
Sucrose	$C_{12}H_{22}O_{11}$	cane sugar	grocery store
Sulfuric acid, dilute	H_2SO_4		chemical supply house
Talc	$H_2Mg_3(SiO_3)_4$	ingredient of talcum powder	drugstore

LABORATORY TECHNIQUES

The handling of laboratory apparatus is a skill you will want to develop. As with any other accomplishment, you will find a great deal of satisfaction in mastering it. It will help you to do your experiments more easily and more efficiently. Neatness and cleanliness are very important in a laboratory. Arrange the shelves above your table to suit your own convenience, but after every experiment, be sure to return each piece of equipment to its proper place. Keep all metal and glassware clean and dry. Keep the outside of your "stock" bottles clean and free of any chemical substance. Replace worn or torn boxes at once. Label everything in your laboratory correctly and legibly. CAUTION: If you use kitchen utensils in your laboratory, make sure your mother doesn't want to use them anymore. Even if they're washed, it isn't safe to cook with them after they have held chemicals.

How to Use an Alcohol Burner.

Many experiments require heat, and the alcohol burner is more efficient for this purpose than a candle. Keep the wick clean and trimmed.

Whenever the flame is not blue, it is either because the wick is dirty or needs trimming. When you are not using the burner, keep it tightly covered to prevent evaporation of the alcohol. In lighting the burner, strike the match away from you. In putting it out, cover it quickly with the metal cap. After you refill it and before you strike a match, make sure that no spilled alcohol remains on the outside of the jar, on the table, or in your hands.

How to Cut Glass Tubing.

With the sharp edge of a triangular file, scratch one line on the tubing, at the exact point where you wish to cut it. Now place your thumbs on each side of the scratch and break the tubing quickly by forcing it away from you. The diameter of the tubing makes no difference; the method is the same.

How to Fire-Polish Glass.

The rough edges of glass tubing make it awkward to use as well as dangerous. If the edges are very rough, rub them back and forth on a piece of wire screening to remove the largest "splinters." Do this over a piece of newspaper. When you have finished, fold the newspaper carefully and throw it away. Now light the alcohol burner and place one end of the tubing in the blue flame, holding the other end with your hand. The flame will become bright orange. Rotate the tubing between your thumb and forefinger until the edge in the flame is rounded. Place this end on an asbestos pad until it has cooled and repeat the process on the other end. CAUTION: If you keep the glass in the flame for too long, it will melt, the hole will close, and you will have a closed tube instead of an open one.

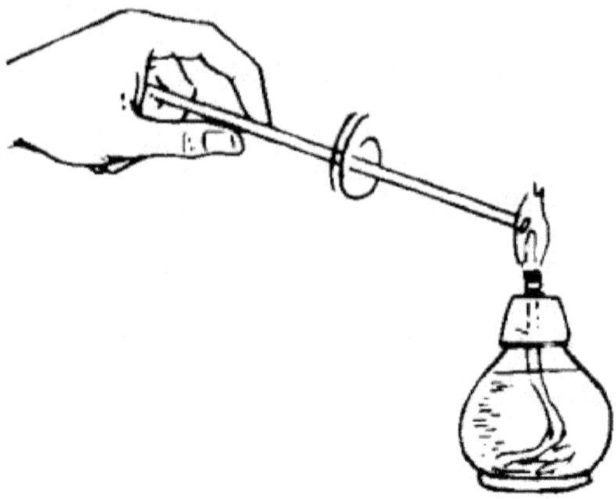

How to Bend Glass.

Put the flame spreader, or "fishtail tip" over the wick of your alcohol burner. Holding a piece of glass tubing in both hands, one on either side of the flame, rotate the glass until the bright orange color appears in the flame. Remove the tubing from the flame and bend it quickly to the de-sired angle. If you want a particular angle or special shape, draw it first on paper. When the glass is ready for bending, hold it an inch above the paper and follow your drawing like a pattern. CAUTION: Remember the glass is very hot and may cause the paper to smolder if it touches it.

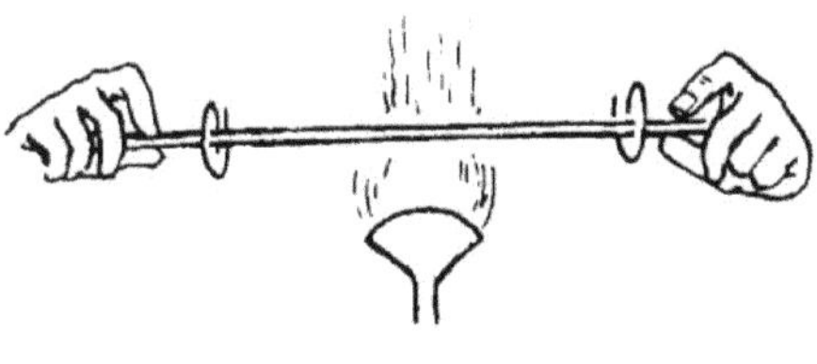

How to Stretch Glass.

Do not use the fishtail tip on the burner. Hold the glass and roll it in the flame with both hands. When the bright orange color appears, push the ends of the tube together so that the walls of the tube become a little thicker. Remove the glass from the flame and pull the ends of the tube apart. Try to keep your hands and the tube in a straight line. To make a nozzle or a dropper, cut the glass to the length you want and fire-polish each tip.

How to Handle Powdered

Chemicals and Crystals. If the stopper is hollow, turn the bottle on its side and rotate it with one hand until some of the contents are inside the stopper. Remove the stopper in such a manner that the chemical remains in it, but none falls from the mouth of the bottle. Gently tap the stopper with your index finger until the correct amount has fallen out. Replace the stopper.

Using a spatula, shovel out a little of the dry material. Tap the blade of the spatula with your index finger as you did the stopper.

To transfer a chemical from a bottle to a small jar or beaker, remove the stopper from the bottle, tip the bottle and rotate it over the desired container until the proper amount is in the new container.

How to Remove the Stopper from a Bottle of Liquid Chemical.

Holding the stopper in place with one hand, tip the bottle so that the stopper becomes wet with the liquid. Now hold the bottle upright, and, using the stopper, wet the edge of the bottle. Replace the stopper and remove it again between your third and fourth fingers. Keep your palm facing upward, and grasp the bottle in the same hand, between your thumb and first two fingers. By using the same hand to pour the liquid, your other hand remains free to hold additional equipment.

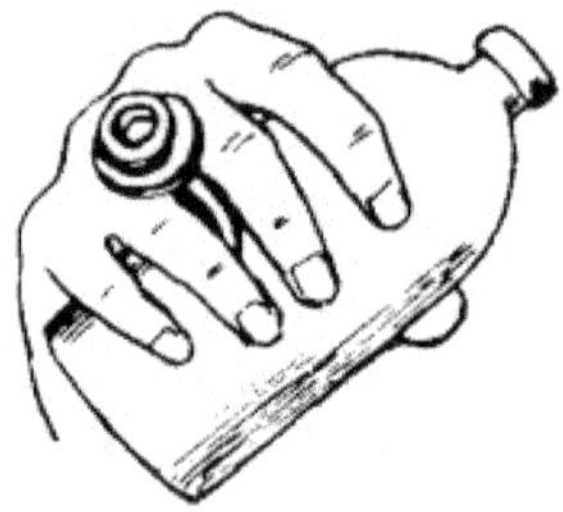

How to Pour a Liquid Chemical.

If you have removed the stopper properly, the wet edge of the bottle will prevent the liquid from rushing out too quickly. Now place a glass rod across the mouth of the tilted bottle, and pour the liquid down the rod. The rod acts to direct the flow.

How to Use an Eye Dropper.

Never use an eyedropper to remove a liquid directly from a bottle. First, pour a small quantity of the liquid into a beaker, then use the eyedropper. To transfer the liquid to a test tube containing another substance, do not plunge the eyedropper into the chemical in the test tube unless instructed to do so. Instead, hold the dropper near the top of the test tube and let the drops run down the inside of the tube.

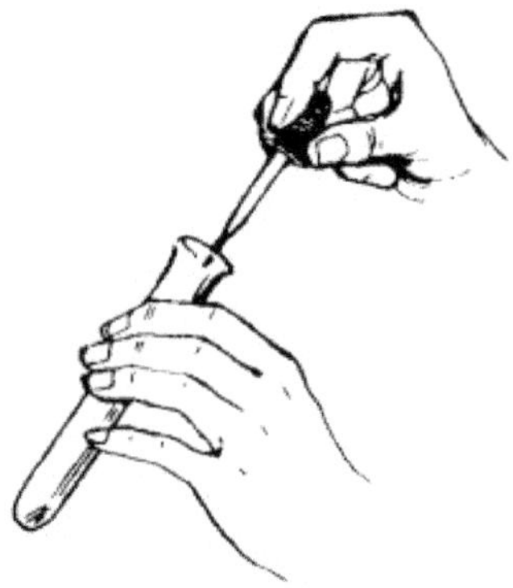

How to Measure a ·Liquid.

If you look through the side of a measuring glass filled with a liquid, you will see that the surface of the liquid has a double curve. This curve is called the meniscus. In measuring, be sure to use the lowest part of the lower. curve.

Most liquids have a concave meniscus (one that curves downward) but very dense liquids like mercury have a convex meniscus (one that curves upward). In that case, use the uppermost part of the upper curve for measuring.

How to Use Filter Paper.

Fold a circle of filter paper in half and then into quarters. Open it so that it becomes cone-shaped. Roughly tear off one corner. Place the filter paper in a funnel and fill it with water. Let the water run through until there is no air in the stem, then stop the flow with your finger. Now add the liquid mixture to be filtered. The presence of liquid rather than air in the stem makes the other liquid, that is, the mixture, pour through more quickly.

Siphoning.

When you have to transfer a liquid from one jar or beaker to another without disturbing the liquid by tilting the jar to pour from it, you use the technique of siphoning. You need two containers, of course, and a long tube. Use a rubber tube which will bend easily, not a glass tube. Place the containers on two different surfaces. The container to be filled should be on a surface lower than the bottom of the container to be emptied.

Submerge the tube in the upper container so that it is completely filled with liquid. Keep one end of the tube submerged and, holding the other end closed, lower it into the empty container. When you open the tube, the liquid will flow.

The Statistical Method.

All this really means is that the more times you repeat a particular experiment, the better basis you will have for predicting the result of that experiment in the future. The first time you experiment, you cannot really tell whether you would get the same result if you were to repeat it. But, if you did the same experiment 10 times and got the same result every time, you would then be fairly safe in predicting that that experiment will continue to produce the same result whenever it is done. In other words, the margin of error of your prediction would go down the more times you repeated the experiment and got the same result. If, on the other hand, you got 10 different results, your margin of error would go up, and any prediction you might make would be meaningless.

Professional scientists always use the statistical method. They know that they cannot leap to conclusions based on a single experiment. The only way to be sure that particular conditions produce a particular result is to repeat an experiment over and over again. In science, being "sure" means being able to predict with only a small margin of error that particular conditions will produce particular results. Accurate predictions can be made on one basis only-repeated experiments.

SAFETY RULES

Your laboratory is not a place to play. Experimenting is a serious business, and you have to carry it out in a businesslike way if you are to learn anything from it. The rules below will help you to enjoy your experiments and learn from them without endangering yourself or others.

Do not allow your friends to mix things just to see what will happen. Do not do so yourself. Some combinations of chemicals are dangerous and you might accidentally mix some of these. Perform only the experiments for which you have complete instructions.

Always keep a good supply of tap water on your laboratory table. Unless you are working near a sink, have a wide-mouthed gallon jar filled with water close at hand, as well as several large sponges for wiping up any chemicals that might be spilled.

If an acid or an alkali (base) is spilled on your clothing, skin or any place in your laboratory, immediately wash the area with lots of clear water.

An American Red Cross first-aid handbook should be part of your laboratory equipment.

Refer to it in case of an accident, and never hesitate to call a doctor if you are accidentally burned or inhale irritating fumes.

Be very careful of hot glass. It doesn't look hot and it cools very slowly.

Treat burns at once with sodium bicarbonate solution. Never put hot glassware down on an unprotected table.

When heating chemicals or chemical solutions in a test tube, do not point the open end toward yourself or anyone else. Keep rotating the test tube constantly with a gentle circular motion so that bubbles forming rapidly in the bottom of the test tube will not force the liquid out of the tube in a dangerous way.

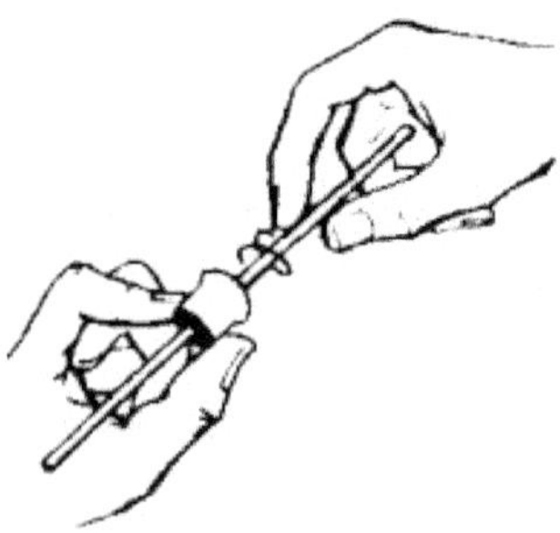

Before using glass tubing, be sure that both ends are fire-polished.

To put the tube through a cork or rubber stopper, wet it first. Hold it with a piece of cloth and insert it gently into the hole by rotating it while you apply pressure. Once you have started the tubing through a stopper, never hold the tube from a point more than 2 inches away from the stopper. Otherwise, the weight of the stopper will make the tube snap. If the tubing is part of a funnel or thistle tube, do not hold it by the funnel for the same reason. Handle thermometers the same way, too.

Never use a chemical that is not labeled. It might be poisonous or cause a violent and dangerous reaction. Never return unused chemicals to their original bottles. You may cause contamination or make an error that will spoil future experiments. Throw the unused chemical away in the proper waste container.

Only waste paper belongs in the wastepaper basket. Put discarded solid chemicals in an earthen or pottery jar. Later you should wrap them in newspaper and throw them in an incinerator or garbage can. Put liquid wastes into a sink partly filled with water, and then wash them away with the tap water running for at least

5 minutes. This will dilute them and lessen the effect they might otherwise have on the plumbing.

Never taste or smell a chemical directly. Do not do so at all unless the experiment directs you to. To taste a chemical, transfer I drop to your tongue using a glass rod. Wash your mouth out immediately with water. To smell a chemical, fan the vapor toward your nose with your hand. Be prepared to turn your head away quickly if the odor proves to be irritating.

Keep glass apparatus spotlessly clean. Contamination often spoils the results of experiments. When you wet clean glass, it takes on an even coating of water, but on dirty glass, the water forms small droplets instead. You can use any good detergent for cleaning, but be sure to rinse the apparatus thoroughly afterward.

Always wear a rubber or plastic apron to protect your clothing when doing experiments; unless you already wear eyeglasses, you should have a pair of plastic goggles or safety glasses to protect your eyes whenever this is suggested in a particular experiment. Asbestos gloves are a good safety factor for experiments involving fire.

CHEMICALS IN THE AIR

Perhaps you know that air is a mixture of many gases and that we live at the bottom of a great ocean of it. You've probably heard this or similar statements before. But what do you know about the gases the air is made of? First, the combination of gases in the air forms a mixture. Like a compound, a mixture contains two or more different substances. But in a mixture, the substances are not combined chemically. The proportions of different substances in a mixture may vary from place to place and from time to time; they can also be separated from each other more easily than the different substances in a compound.

The mixture called air contains molecules of nitrogen (N2), oxygen (02), carbon dioxide (C02), water vapor (H 20), and the *inert gases*: helium (He), radon (Rn), argon (A), neon (Ne), krypton (Kr) and xenon (Xe). The air contains more nitrogen than anything; about 78 percent of the air is nitrogen. It is a very inactive (chemists say *inert*) gas, and so the quantity of it in its pure form hardly ever varies. Pure oxygen, which is the most important to us because we use it for breathing, makes up only about 20 percent of the air. Oxygen is an active element and even though there are more atoms of oxygen on earth than of any other kind, they are usually found in combination with other elements rather than as oxygen alone. Oxygen combines easily with many substances and is constantly doing so, so that the quantity of it in the air does vary slightly.

Carbon dioxide in the air is only a small percentage of the mixture compared with the other gases in the air, but the amount of it varies to a much greater degree.

The percentage of water vapor also varies greatly.

What accounts for the changes in the percentage of water vapor and carbon dioxide in the air? A few examples will make this clear. Where would you expect to find more moisture-in a forest, or a desert? In a forest of course. But why?

One reason is that there are so many plants and trees in a forest. When plants grow, they absorb water from the ground. Some of it becomes part of the plant, but a great deal of water is given off into the atmosphere through "pores" in the leaves. This yielding of moisture to the air does not occur in the desert, because there are so few plants there. The few plants that do thrive in the desert don't yield much moisture either. To survive they have evolved in such a way as to prevent the escape of whatever precious moisture they contain. In places where the atmosphere is moist, it usually rains. Where the atmosphere is dry, it does not rain.

The percentage of carbon dioxide varies for a very different reason. Can you guess why the air in industrial cities contains more carbon dioxide than the air in the countryside? One of the products of combustion (burning) is carbon dioxide and the quantity of fuels burned in factories, homes, cars, trucks, and buses gives off much carbon dioxide. The absence of vegetation in cities is another reason for the high percentage of carbon dioxide in the city air. Plants remove a great deal of carbon dioxide from the air during the process of photosynthesis. This is the process by which plants use sunlight to manufacture plant food out of water and minerals.

HOW YOU CAN MEASURE THE PROPORTION OF OXYGEN IN AIR

Gather these materials: A large cork; a small candle; a tall thin glass; a rubber band; a penknife; and a basin containing I inch of water.

Follow this procedure: Slice the cork to get a piece about t of an inch thick, using your penknife. Rotate the cork as you cut it so that you will not have to press very hard. In this way, both the cork and your fingers will be safe. Estimate the center of the circle of cork and attach the candle to that spot with a few drops of candle wax. Now, put it on the surface of the water and see if it will float. To do so, it must be properly balanced. If it isn't, remove the candle and try again. When you have succeeded in making it float, light the candle.

Carefully invert the glass over the floating, lighted candle. Do this in such a way that only the slightest bit of the rim of the glass is underwater. Do not push it down to the bottom of the basin. Watch what happens inside the glass.

When nothing else seems to be happening, slip the rubber band around the glass and let it mark the surface of the water on the inside.

Results: The candle burns for a minute or two and then goes out. As it burns, the water rises in the glass and when it goes out, the water stops rising.

Fires need oxygen to burn. The burning candle used up the oxygen contained in the air in the glass and then went out. Because of the missing oxygen, the air inside the glass became lighter than the air outside the glass. The air outside, therefore, pressed down on the water in the basin more strongly than did the air inside the glass. As a result, it pushed the water up into the glass in proportion to the difference in pressure. This gives you a mathematical way of measuring the amount of oxygen used up. Since all the oxygen originally contained in the air inside the glass was used up, what you are calculating is the proportion of oxygen originally contained in that air.

Suppose your glass was 10 inches tall. Measure the distance between the rim and the position of the rubber band. It should be about 2 inches. That means that oxygen accounted for 2/10 or 1/5 of the original air in the glass. Since 1/5 is 20 percent, you can see that 20 percent of the air was oxygen.

HOW YOU CAN SHOW THAT THE GAS YOU EXHALE CONTAINS CARBON DIOXIDE

Gather these materials: Powdered calcium hydroxide ($Ca(OH)_2$); 1 test tube ¾ filled with water and 1 empty test tube; an alcohol burner; and a drinking straw.

Follow this procedure: Place ½ teaspoonful of calcium hydroxide in the test tube containing the water. Light the alcohol burner and heat the test tube gently until all the powder dissolves, or until no more will dissolve. If it does dissolve completely, add a little more. Set the tube aside to cool; as it cools, the excess calcium hydroxide will settle to the bottom. When the calcium hydroxide has cooled and settled, pour 2 inches of the clear liquid above it into the other test tube. Now blow into the clear liquid through the straw. Continue to do this for 3 minutes. Now light a match and blow it out with your breath.

Results: As soon as your breath touches the solution of calcium hydroxide, the solution begins to turn a milky white. As you continue, it becomes even cloudier. If you now allow the solution to stand, a white precipitate will settle down. A precipitate is an insoluble substance that separates out from a solution as the result of certain types of chemical reactions.

Calcium hydroxide solution provides the chemical test for carbon dioxide, which makes it turn milky white. No other gas, when bubbled into it, will make it do that and make it afterward form this white precipitate. The equation for this reaction is as follows (the arrow pointing downward shows that a precipitate was formed):

$$CO_2 + Ca(OH)_2 \longrightarrow CaCO_3 \downarrow + H_2O$$

The match you lit went out immediately when you blew on it. Fires cannot burn without oxygen. Since carbon dioxide is a heavy gas, it lies close to the burning object and keeps out the oxygen-containing air. This is why your breath, which contains carbon dioxide, extinguished the match.

HOW TO MAKE A FIRE EXTINGUISHER

Gather these materials: A l-holed rubber stopper; a milk bottle; a glass tube about one inch shorter than the milk bottle, stretched at one end to form a nozzle; a small, narrow perfume bottle; a 6-inch string; sodium bicarbonate ($NaHCO_3$) and acetic acid (CH_3COOH).

Follow this procedure: Fill the milk bottle halfway with water. Add 3 teaspoonfuls of sodium bicarbonate to it. Tie a string around the neck of the perfume bottle. Fill the perfume bottle with acetic acid. Suspend the perfume bottle in the milk bottle, letting the string hang over the rim of the milk bottle and hold the string so the bottle doesn't drop. Put the glass tubing into the rubber stopper and the stopper into the milk bottle. The stopper will hold the string in place.

In case of fire, turn the milk bottle upside down over the flames.

Results: When you turn the bottle upside down, the acetic acid and the sodium bicarbonate solution are brought into contact. They react to produce carbon dioxide, which comes out from the glass tube onto the fire. This extinguisher is effective, but only for very small fires.

HOW WATER VAPOR BEHAVES IN AIR: THE RAIN CYCLE

There is a continuous rain cycle on earth. Today in New York it may be clear and sunny, but at the same time tomorrow, it may rain. Similarly, a cloudy or foggy day in Chicago today might be a dry, sparkling day tomorrow. These changes come about because the water in the atmosphere and on earth is always changing its state of matter, that is, from solid (ice) to liquid (water) to gas (water vapor). It collects as a liquid in bodies of water on earth. Warmed by the sun, some of it evaporates and rises into the atmosphere, where it cools and condenses. As the condensed water droplets gather together, they form clouds, and when the clouds get heavy enough, the water droplets spill to earth as rain, snow, hail, or sleet- the main kinds of *precipitation*. The bodies of water on earth then fill up again, and the cycle starts anew.

THE CHEMISTRY OF WATER

Water is one of the simplest compounds and one of the commonest on earth.

Indeed, more of the earth's surface is covered by water than by land. The human body itself is made up mostly of water. That is one of the reasons why water is so essential to life, along with food and air.

Water has always fascinated men, but it was only in the relatively recent past that they discovered what it really was. The ancient Greeks thought there were only four elements and that water was one. Earth, fire and air were the other substances they mistakenly called elements. Until the end of the 18th century, everyone, including the most learned men, accepted this theory. Today of course we know that none of these "elements" is really an element at all.

We know that water is a compound of hydrogen and oxygen and that the same compound can exist as a solid (ice), a liquid (water) or a gas (water vapor). It appears most commonly as a liquid, however, because that is its state of matter within the temperature range of 32 to 212 o Fahrenheit.

In the following section, you will discover for yourself that water consists of hydrogen and oxygen, how the water drawn into cities from lakes and rivers is made fit to drink and what makes water "hard" or "soft."

HOW YOU CAN DECOMPOSE WATER BY ELECTROLYSIS

Gather these materials: Two pieces of copper wire 12 inches long and 2 pieces 4 inches long; 2 dry cells; sodium chloride (NaCI); 2 strips of aluminum foil, ½ by 3 inches in size; 2 test tubes; and a quart glass jar or any wide-mouthed container.

Follow this procedure: 1. Look at the diagram on page 35 and arrange your materials in the same way. If you follow these directions carefully and check each step with the diagram, you will have no trouble. Set up your apparatus in exactly this way:

Attach one strip of aluminum foil to one end of a 12-inch length of copper wire.

Connect the free end of the copper wire to thc ccntral terminal of one dry cell.

Attach one end of a 4-inch piece of copper wire to the outside terminal of the same dry cell.

Attach the free end of this 4-inch piece of wire to the central terminal of the second dry cell.

Attach one end of the second 12-inch piece of wire to the outside terminal of the second dry cell.

Attach the second piece of aluminum foil to the free end of this 12-inch piece of wire.

Now fill the quart glass jar with water. To make it conduct electricity, add to it ½ teaspoonful of sodium chloride. Insert the strips of aluminum foil as the diagram shows and cover each one with a test tube filled with water. Let the apparatus stand undisturbed. At the end of 1-½ hours, observe the test tubes.

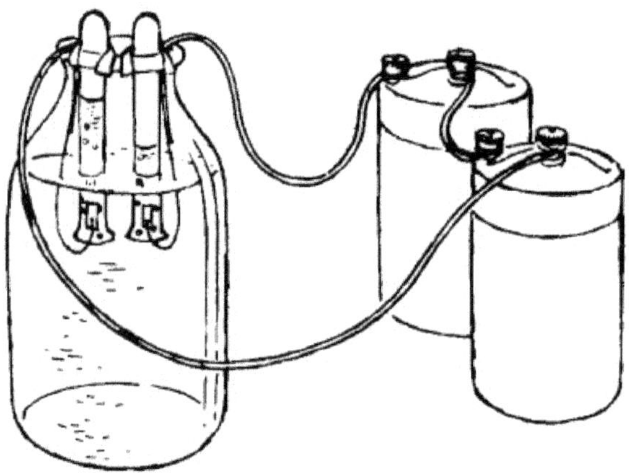

Results: Bubbles of gas began to appear and collected around each of the strips of aluminum foil. The gas collected at the top of each test tube by the principle of Downward Displacement of Water. The amount of gas in one test tube was about twice that in the other test tube.

2. Perform these chemical tests to determine what gases are in the test tubes.

First, light a wooden splint and extinguish the flame, allowing the tip to glow.

Put the glowing splint into the test tube with less gas. Then perform the same test with the other test tube, but be very cautious. Hold the test tube upside down, and with its mouth pointing away from you, put a glowing splint close to the opening.

Results: When you put the glowing splint into the first test tube, it burst into a bright white flame. Oxygen supports combustion, so this proves that the gas in the test tube was oxygen. When you put the glowing splint near the opening of the second test tube, there was a "pop"-the sound of a small explosion. This proves that the gas was hydrogen. There should also be some moisture inside the test tube. This is additional proof that the gas was hydrogen because when hydrogen explodes, it unites with oxygen in air to form water.

So now you have established that the two gases you collected were hydrogen and oxygen, and there was twice as much hydrogen as oxygen. The electrical current broke down or decomposed the molecules of water into their constituent parts-2 atoms of hydrogen and 1 atom of oxygen. The electrical method of *decomposing* a substance is known as electrolysis. The equation for the reaction in this experiment is:

$$2H_2O \rightleftarrows 2H_2 + O_2$$

HOW WATER IS MADE FIT TO DRINK

In the different phases of the water cycle, waterfalls to different places. As it falls on different kinds of rock or runs underground through different types of soil, different chemicals-mainly minerals-dissolve in it.

The chemicals that are dissolved in our drinking water give it its very special taste. Did you ever have the experience of visiting another city or spending the summer in the country, and noticing that the water tasted different? This was because minerals which you were not accustomed to were dissolved in that water.

Many things can make water unfit to drink. Some minerals that dissolve in it, like sulfur, give it an unpleasant taste. Some give it a sickening odor. Sometimes industrial plants produce chemical wastes that find their way into the drinking water. Many harmful bacteria (microscopic plants, sometimes called germs) live in water. Each community is responsible for providing pure water for its citizens. How do they do it? And how can they do it economically?

There are six basic ways of removing all the unpleasant and unsafe materials that find their way into drinking water. Most towns and cities use a combination of these methods that are best suited to their particular situation.

Boiling. The most dangerous types of contaminants in water are bacteria. All bacteria do not cause disease, but many of them do. Since they are too small to be seen with the naked eye, you can't tell just by looking at water whether it contains bacteria, harmful or otherwise. Boiling kills almost all germs, but it is an impractical method of purifying water, except in small amounts. You don't have to worry about bacteria in water from the tap because it has already been purified by other methods. When you camp out, though, and take water from a lake or stream, you should always boil it before drinking it.

Filtering. Some of the contaminants in water are solid, inanimate particles. These don't necessarily make people sick, but they are unpleasant. If you live near the Mississippi River, for example, you would certainly not want to drink its water in the springtime. Then it is full of small dirt particles and is muddy.

In a laboratory, solid particles can be separated from a liquid by using filter paper. In a large town or city, however, sand and gravel beds are used to filter out solids from the water. Gravel and sand are the same except that gravel consists of much larger, coarser particles.

Coagulation. In this process, potassium aluminum sulfate is added to the water before it is filtered. This makes many tiny particles group themselves together so they are large enough to be filtered out in huge tanks called filter beds or settling tanks. Coagulation is used in areas where the solid particle contaminants of clay in the water are very small. It is also used in large cities to remove the remains of germs which have already been killed by other means, but which are too small to be filtered out using sand or gravel alone.

Chlorination. Chlorine kills disease-causing germs in water chemically, but you would have to go to a biological laboratory to perform experiments proving this. You would have to grow cultures (colonies grown in a test tube) of harmful bacteria and then kill them with chlorine. Both these things would be much too dangerous and too difficult to do at home. Furthermore, chlorine, in sufficiently large amounts, is a poisonous gas and very dangerous to work with. By adding a chlorine solution to water, many cities and towns ensure the safety of their citizens from disease-causing germs in the water. During the war, servicemen became familiar with little pills called halazone tablets. These tablets, which contained a chlorine compound, halazone, very effectively killed all harmful bacteria in the unpurified water the men often had to drink. You are probably familiar with the smell and taste of chlorine because it is often added to the water in swimming pools.

Aeration. In a water system that uses this method, there are huge nozzles near the reservoirs that spray the water into the air as if they were tremendous fountains. As the nozzles break the water into small droplets, they also expose it to air, which improves its flavor and removes unpleasant odors. This method of purifying water is used when large quantities of water are involved and in places where the natural taste and odor of the water are unpleasant.

Distillation. Distilled water is the only kind of water that is 100 percent chemically pure H2O. Distillation occurs in two stages: evaporation and condensation. After distillation, no contaminants of any kind remain in the water. Water goes through a natural distillation process every time it evaporates from the sea and then condenses into clouds. Rainwater, therefore, is always pure if it doesn't fall through dirty air.

HOW YOU CAN SHOW THAT SAND AND GRAVEL ARE USEFUL IN FILTERING

Gather these materials: Three funnels; an upright stand and 3 ring supports; pieces of gauze; 3-pint jars; sand from a nearby beach or sandpit; soil from the backyard or garden; gravel from the driveway of your home, from some nearby area, or a pet shop.

Follow this procedure: Arrange the upright stand and ring supports as shown in the diagram. Place a funnel containing a piece of gauze in each one. In the first funnel put 1 inch of ordinary soil; in the second put 1 inch of sand; and in the third put 1 inch of gravel. Pour 1 cupful of very muddy water slowly through each funnel, and catch the water that goes through each in separate pint jars. Compare the results.

Results: The amount of mud that came through each filter differed. The gravel, which permitted the most mud to get through, was the least effective filter. If the soil you used as a filter contained clay, then the mud not only passed through it but also dragged some of the clay with it. The sand did the best job of filtering out the solid particles. Large cities filter water through sand in filter beds or settling tanks. The water still needs further treatment, though, because even though it is clear, it is not necessarily free from germs or pleasant to the taste.

HOW YOU CAN OBSERVE COAGULATION

Gather these materials: Powdered potassium aluminum sulfate ($AI_2(So_4)_3\ K_2So_4$); a small amount of clay; some sand; 2 funnels; filter paper; an upright stand and 2 ring supports; and 4-pint jars.

Follow this procedure: Arrange the stand, ring supports, and funnels lined with filter paper as shown in the diagram. Put about I inch of sand in each of the funnels. Mix 2/3 of a cupful of water and 2 teaspoonfuls of clay in one jar.

Make a similar mixture in the other jar, but add also 2 teaspoonfuls of potassium aluminum sulfate. Stir both mixtures. Pour each mixture through a different funnel into clean pint jars. Compare the liquids that you catch in the pint jars.

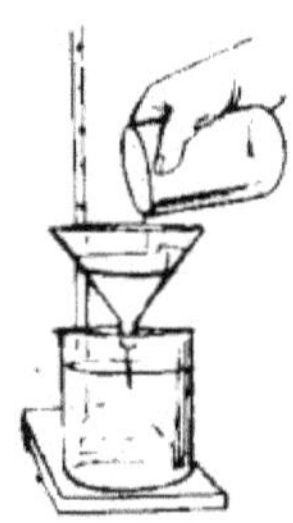

Results: The potassium aluminum sulfate made the small particles of clay stick together so that they filtered out as if they were much larger. The particles in the liquid without the potassium aluminum sulfate got through the filter much more easily. In places where the water passes through a clayey type of soil, the water department uses this process.

HOW YOU CAN DISTILL WATER

Gather these materials: A pyrex flask; a l-holed rubber stopper or cork; a 10-inch piece of glass tubing; a clean pint jar; a large pot or bowl that will easily hold the pint jar; a trayful of ice cubes; a glass rod; an alcohol burner; an upright stand and clamp; 3 cups; copper sulfate crystals ($CuSO_4$); sodium chloride (NaCl); and sucrose ($C_{12}H_{22}O_{11}$)

Follow this procedure: Mix ¼ cup of water with I teaspoonful of sucrose. Mix ¼ cup of water with 1 teaspoonful of sodium chloride. Mix ¼ cup of warm water with 1 teaspoonful of copper sulfate crystals. Note the color of the third solution. Now pour all three solutions into the pyrex flask. Arrange the apparatus as the diagram shows. You will have to bend the glass tubing in two places. Put some ice cubes into the pot or bowl and add some water. This will keep the temperature at a more constant level. Then put the pint jar into the bowl. Place the alcohol burner under the flask, and bring the mixture to a slow boil.

Allow most of the liquid to boil away. Note the color of the liquid collected in the jar.

Results: As the liquid boiled, the color became darker. As it evaporated, steam formed and the quantity of water in the flask decreased. The steam went through the glass tubing to the pint jar embedded in ice. The sudden temperature change made the steam condense into water. The water in the jar was colorless.

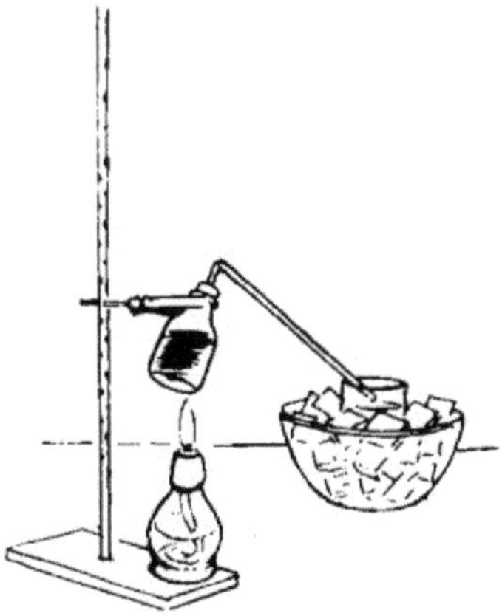

In distillation, evaporation occurs first. This means that when the boiling liquid reached 2lr F., the boiling point of water, the molecules of water jumped off the surface in the form of invisible water vapor. When these molecules reached the ice-cold jar, their temperature quickly went down, and they changed back to liquid water. All the molecules of sodium chloride, sucrose, and copper sulfate remained in the flask.

Each of these substances evaporates at a different temperature, and all of their evaporating temperatures are much higher than that of water. This makes distillation an easy way to separate solid contaminants from water. Unfortunately, the process would be too slow and too expensive to use in large cities, where enormous quantities of purified water are needed.

Distilled water is used in filling medical prescriptions, in batteries, in steam irons, and wherever else lOO percent chemically pure water is required.

HOW YOU CAN CHANGE HARD WATER TO SOFT WATER

Gather these materials: Distilled water (H_2O); ordinary tap water (H_2O with impurities); soap; calcium bicarbonate ($Ca(HCO_3)_2$); magnesium sulfate ($MgSO_4$); sodium tetraborate ($Na_2B_4O_7$) or potassium carbonate (K_2CO_3); 6 test tubes; a test tube rack; a test tube holder; an alcohol burner; a quart jar; and an eyedropper.

Follow this procedure: Make a soap solution by soaking some soap in a quart jar filled with water. Then prepare a data sheet similar to the one below, and fill in the information as you experiment:

Test Tube No.	***Contents of Tube***	***Treatment***	***Conclusion***
1	distilled water	added soap solution, shook tube after each drop, counted drops	drops needed to make suds

Set up the test tubes in the test tube rack and label them 1 to 6. As you experiment, add to the labels the names of the things you put into the test tubes. Fill the tubes according to these directions: No.1, distilled water; No.2, tap water; No.3, water and 1 teaspoonful of calcium bicarbonate; No.4, same as No.3; No.5, water and 1 teaspoonful of magnesium sulfate; No.6, same as No.5.

With the eyedropper, add some soap solution, drop by drop, to test tube No. 1, shaking the tube very hard between drops. Count how many drops are needed to make suds and record the number. To test tube No.2, add some soap solution in the same manner and count again. To test tube No.3, add some soap solution in the same way. Take test tube No.4 from the rack and boil the liquid over the alcohol flame. Add some soap solution after it has cooled, and count the drops needed to form suds. To test tube No.5 add soap solution only, shake, count the drops, and record the result. To test tube No.6 add 1 teaspoonful of sodium tetraborate or potassium carbonate, then add some soap solution, shake, count the drops, and record the result. By now you have a great deal of information on your datasheet. Compare all your results.

Results: Distilled water (test tube No.1) made suds very easily and didn't require many drops of soap solution or much shaking. Tap water (test tube No.2) made suds easily or else not at all, depending upon what part of the country you live in. The more minerals dissolved in your water, the less easily suds form. The calcium bicarbonate solution (test tube No.3) made very few suds, and those that it did make disappeared very quickly. The other calcium bicarbonate solution (test tube No.4) made very good suds after you boiled it and after a white precipitate separated out. The magnesium sulfate solution (test tube No.5) formed few suds. The other magnesium sulfate solution (test tube No.6) made goods suds after you added sodium tetraborate or potassium carbonate.

You have been experimenting with four different kinds of water. Distilled water is chemically pure H_2O. Because it contains no impurities, it makes soap suds very easily. Tap water is hard or soft, depending on whether there are many minerals in the soil near your home or near the source of water for your city.

If it made no suds or poor suds, then it contained many minerals and consequently was hard. Bicarbonates dissolved in water make a special kind of hard water called temporary hard water. You can soften this type of hard water simply by boiling it, as you did. The equation showing how the impurity was forced out as a precipitate is:

$$Ca(HCO_3)_2 \xrightarrow{\Delta} CaCO_3\downarrow + H_2O + CO_2\uparrow$$

Remember that an arrow pointing upward indicates a gas that has been released and an arrow pointing down indicates a precipitate. The Greek letter delta over the arrow shows heat. Magnesium sulfate also makes water hard, but you can't soften this type of hard water by boiling it. You must add another chemical to react with the sulfate impurity which prevents the soap from forming suds. Sodium tetraborate and potassium carbonate are chemicals that will do this. Here are the equations showing how they act:

$$MgSO_4 + Na_2B_4O_7 \rightarrow MgB_4O_7 + Na_2SO_4$$

$$MgSO_4 + K_2CO_3 \rightarrow MgCO_3 + KSO_4$$

For industrial use, large quantities of water are softened by adding a zeolite, a special compound for softening water.

THE CHEMISTRY OF SOLUTIONS, DIFFUSION AND OSMOSIS

When salt (NaCl) or sugar ($C_{12}H_{22}O_{11}$) dissolves in water, the water remains clear and colorless but tastes salty or sweet. When copper sulfate ($CuSO_4$) dissolves in water, the water remains clear but it turns blue. A few drops of ink in a glass of water have a similar effect on the water. A liquid containing another substance dissolved in it is a *solution*, regardless of how much of the other substance or how many different substances are dissolved in it. A solution, therefore, is a clear liquid mixture of two or more substances, the amounts of which may vary. A solution is never lumpy. The liquid in which the substances dissolve is called the *solvent*, and the dissolved substances themselves are *solutes*. A cup of tea then is a solution, in which the solvent is hot water or a mixture of hot water with lemon or milk. The solutes are the sugar and the chemicals from the tea leaves.

Water is sometimes called the "universal solvent" because almost everything dissolves in it, at least a little. Here are some curious facts about solutions.

The higher the temperature of the solvent, the more easily solutions form, and also the greater is the proportion of solute that actually dissolves. This is why sugar dissolves better in hot tea than in iced tea.

Gases are the exception to this rule. They dissolve more easily in cold liquids than in hot ones. This is why soda gets "flat" when you allow it to stand uncapped outside the refrigerator. As the liquid gets warmer, the gas (carbon dioxide) contained in the solution escapes.

The smaller the particles of the solute, the more easily a solution forms.

This is why finely ground sugar is used in iced tea.

When one liquid dissolves in another, the combination in solution occupies less space than either liquid occupied separately. The combination of I quart of water and I quart of alcohol makes less than 2 quarts in solution.

Some of the most vital processes of living creatures depend on the ability of solutions to pass through a very thin type of skin called a *membrane*. This is the process of *osmosis*.

Without osmosis, minerals and water from the soil wouldn't get into plants; oxygen wouldn't get into our blood, and neither would food. But first, the minerals and water in the soil, the oxygen we breathe in, and the food we eat have to be dissolved. The process by which our bodies dissolve the food we eat is *digestion.*

When solid particles fail to dissolve in a liquid, they form a *suspension.* When solid particles seem to dissolve in a liquid, but the "solution" lacks the property of being able to pass through a membrane, it is not really a solution, but a *colloid.* When two liquids don't form a single clear liquid, they form an *emulsion.*

Colloids and emulsions are kinds of *suspensions.*

The ability of one substance to make another substance dissolve in it is very important to the cleaning industry. No amount of soap and water will remove paint stains or chewing gum. But if the cleaner knows what caused the stain, he can remove it with the proper solvent.

WHAT HAPPENS WHEN YOU MIX A SOLID AND A LIQUID

Gather these materials: Sodium chloride (NaCl); talcum powder; copper sulfate ($CuSO_4$); garden soil; sucrose ($C_{12}H_{22}O_{11}$); potassium aluminum sulfate ($AI_2(SO_4)_3.K_2SO_4$); 5 pieces of filter paper; 5 homemade funnels or 1 regular funnel; 10 test tubes; a test tube rack; some warm water; and an alcohol burner.

Follow this procedure: Label 5 test tubes 1 to 5 or label their places in the test tube rack. Fill these 5 test tubes halfway with warm water. Put! Teaspoonful of sodium chloride into the first test tube, 1- teaspoonful of talcum powder into the second, and so on, for the next three substances. Do not use the potassium aluminum sulfate yet. If the substance doesn't dissolve right away, heat the test tube over thc alcohol burner until it does, or until you are sure it won't. Make out a data sheet similar to this one:

Number of	*Substance Put*	*Appearance*	*Appearance*	*Appearance*
Test Tube	*into Test Tube*	*Before Heating*	*After Heating*	*After Filtering*

Arrange a funnel lined with filter paper in each of the remaining 5 test tubes.

Now One by one, filter the "solutions" by pouring them through the funnel into the different test tubes. If you use only one funnel, place it in the remaining 5 test tubes, one after the other, and be sure to use a fresh piece of filter paper every time. Fill in the datasheet. Rinse out the test tube in which you first put the garden soil. Add a small quantity of potassium aluminum sulfate to the test tube containing the filtered garden-soil "solution" and filter it again into the test tube you rinsed out.

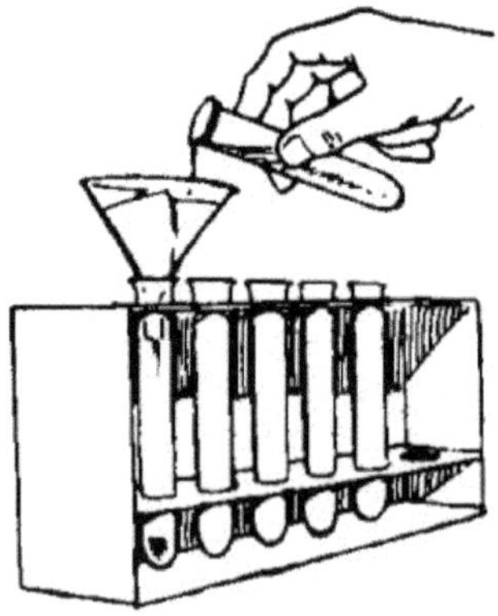

Results: Sodium chloride, sucrose, and copper sulfate pass easily through the filter paper. You can tell that they make true solutions because they leave no residue in the funnel. The filtering separated out the particles of talcum and garden soil. They were not true solutions, therefore. After adding potassium aluminum sulfate and refiltering the water that contained them, even the finer particles of soil, which went through the first time, separated out.

Many cities use the process of adding potassium aluminum sulfate and refiltering to clear up slightly muddy water. This process, which, as you remember from page 37, is called coagulation, depends on the fact that potassium aluminum sulfate makes the fine particles of mud clump together to form larger pieces that do filter out. However, this process cannot remove dissolved industrial wastes. It cannot purify liquid sewage or germ-polluted water either. The liquid sewage contains dissolved impurities, and germs are too small to be filtered out in this particular way.

WHAT HAPPENS WHEN YOU MIX DIFFERENT KINDS OF LIQUIDS

Gather these materials: One small can of concentrated grape juice; salad oil; an alcohol solution of 85 to 90 %strength; 2-pint jars; 2 test tubes; and 3-quart jars fitted with covers.

Follow this procedure: Prepare a data sheet with the following headings:

Water mixed with: *Result*

Fill one-quart jar halfway with water. Measure I full test tube of concentrated grape juice. Add this to the water. Cover the jar and shake it very hard. Record the result. Allow it to stand for a few minutes, and record whether or not any change takes place. Fill the next quart jar halfway with water. Measure I full test tube of salad oil and add it to the water. Cover the jar and shake it. Record the result immediately and again after allowing it to stand for 5 minutes. Fill one-pint jar with water and the other pint jar with alcohol. Pour both into the third-quart jar. Again, cover the jar and shake it. Notice and record the level of the liquid in this jar as well as its appearance.

Results: The grape juice and water mixed with each other very easily. When you allowed them to stand, they did not separate. The water and oil did not mix easily. After shaking the jar very hard, the oil and water seemed to mix together. But when you allowed the mixture to stand, the water and oil soon separated, and the oil came to the top. The alcohol and water seemed to act like grape juice and water. That is, they mixed with each other easily. However, there was one big difference. Two pints in this case did not make I quart.

Some liquids when put together form mixtures, just as some solids do. Neither one of them changes chemically or physically. This is what happened to the water and the juice. When liquids behave this way, they are said to diffuse, and they are called *miscible.* Liquids that will not diffuse with one another, like oil and water, are called *non-miscible.*

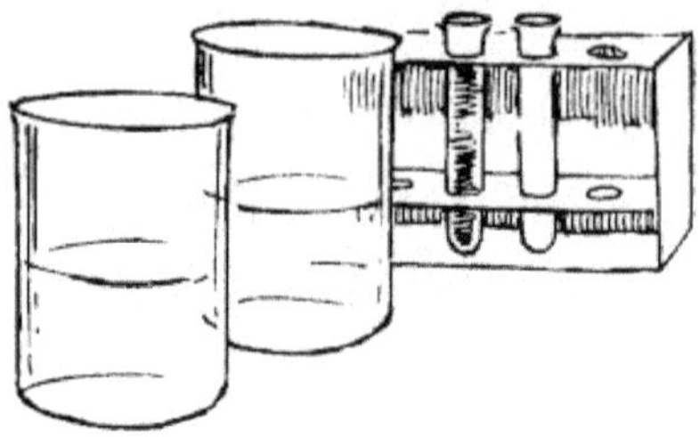 

When you have a product that you know consists of two or more liquids, you can't always tell just by looking if it is a solution or not. Some combinations of non-miscible liquids are made to look like ordinary solutions. At one time people were used to seeing the cream at the top of the milk bottle. The cream and the milk would not mix. Nowadays we buy *homogenized* milk. The cream and milk appear to form only one liquid. Chemists discovered that if they made the particles, or *globules* of butterfat small enough, they would remain afloat in even quantities throughout the milk, even though they still would not actually dissolve in the milk. The milk and cream together form an *emulsion*, a liquid with fatty particles suspended in it.

When two or more liquids form a true solution, they take up less space in the solution than they would separately. Two pints equal I quart-but not if one is water and the other alcohol. When one liquid dissolves in another, the molecules of the solute occupy the empty spaces between the molecules of the solvent. In a liquid, the molecules are fairly far apart. Thus the solution is denser than either substance separately and has less volume than the total volume of the solute and solvent separately.

HOW YOU CAN SEE THE EFFECT OF HEAT ON SOLUTIONS

Gather these materials: Crystalline sodium thiosulfate (Na2S2O3); 3 pyrex jars; a teaspoon; and an alcohol burner.

Follow this procedure: Fill one jar 2/3 full of water at room temperature. Slowly add sodium thiosulfate with the teaspoon until you reach the point where no more will dissolve. Stir the liquid constantly, and keep track of the amount you add so you will know just how much of the chemical dissolved at room temperature. Record this amount. Put the same quantity of water in a second jar and add the same amount of sodium thiosulfate.

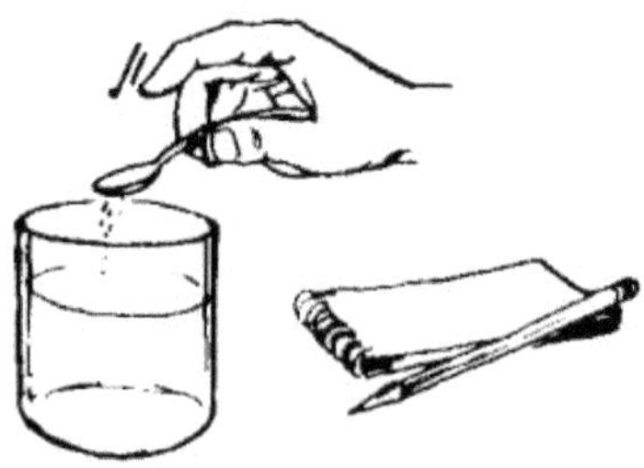

Now heat the solution until small bubbles begin to form, but don't allow it to boil beyond that point. After heating, add more sodium thiosulfate, stirring constantly and keeping track of how much you add. Allow the jar to cool gradually. In the third jar, put the same amount of water and the same total amount of sodium thiosulfate that you added to the second jar. Bring this third solution to a full boil and while it is boiling, add still more sodium thiosulfate. Allow this jar to cool gradually also. When the second and third jars have both cooled to room temperature, put I small crystal of sodium thiosulfate into each of the 3 jars.

Observe the result very closely.

Results: Compared with the other two solutions, the one made at room temperature took relatively little sodium thiosulfate, although it was a true solution. More crystals dissolved when you heated the water, and the greatest amount dissolved when you boiled the water.

The first solution, made at room temperature, was an unsaturated solution. That means it held less solute than it was really capable of holding. Therefore, when you added the extra crystal, it dissolved. The second solution, with heat applied, was a saturated solution. This means that it held all the solute it is normally capable of holding, plus a little excess that didn't dissolve. Therefore, when you later added an extra crystal, it didn't dissolve but fell to the bottom with the other excess undissolved crystals. The third solution, made at boiling temperature, was a supersaturated solution. The boiling forced it to absorb much more solute than it would normally hold. The extra crystal that you later added seemed to be the center of an area where new crystals of sodium thiosulfate grew. Of course, they were not really new. They separated out from the solution as it cooled, and they would have done so even if you hadn't added another crystal. The one you added merely served as a seed crystal, or "starter" for the others to cluster around. The crystal growth continued until the solution was only saturated rather than supersaturated.

You can repeat this experiment with any crystalline chemical, but you will have the best success with crystals that normally contain water of crystallization, such as copper sulfate, because they dissolve more readily.

HOW TO SEPARATE SOLUTES FROM SOLVENTS

Gather these materials: Sodium chloride ($NaCl$); magnesium sulfate ($MgSO_4$); crushed aspirin ($CH_3COOC_6H_4COOH$); boric acid (H_3BO_3); powdered calcium hydroxide ($Ca(OH_2$); sucrose ($C_{12}H_{22}O_{11}$); copper sulfate ($CuSO_4$); grain alcohol (C_2H_5OH); warm water; 8 test tubes; a test tube rack; a test tube holder; a glass rod; an alcohol burner; and paper and pencil.

Follow this procedure: Take a tiny pinch of each powdered or crystalline chemical and taste it. Then put ½ teaspoonful of sodium chloride in the first test tube,½ teaspoonful of magnesium sulfate in the second test tube, and so on until you have ½ teaspoonful of one powdered or crystalline chemical in each of the first 7 test tubes. Then put I teaspoonful of alcohol into the eighth test tube. Now add I tablespoonful of water to the contents of each test tube. Taste a speck of the alcohol and water.

Write in the data for the first three entries of a datasheet, drawn up like this:

No. of Test Tube	1	2	3	4	5	6	7	8
Contents	NaCl	$MgSO_4$	$CH_3COOC_6H_4COOH$	H_3BO_3	$Ca(OH)_2$	$C_{12}H_{22}O_{11}$	$CuSO_4$	C_2H_5OH
Appearance before dissolving								
Description of taste								
Appearance of solution								
Appearance after evaporation								
Description of taste								

Gently heat each tube in turn over the alcohol burner until its contents begin to boil. CAUTION: Remember to keep the mouth of the tube pointed away from your face and at a slight angle. Continue to boil each one, except the eighth one until all the water is gone. As it disappears from each one, taste the residue. Then fill in the rest of the columns on your datasheet. When you reach the eighth tube, boil until only! of an inch of liquid remains. Let it cool slightly and taste it. Fill in the final entries for the alcohol. Now, for each substance, compare all the data about appearance and taste.

Results: Some of these substances dissolved more readily than others, but they all dissolved when the temperature increased enough. Each solution was clear and colorless, except the copper sulfate solution, which was clear and blue. After the first seven solutions evaporated, crystals remained in the tubes. It was the water that evaporated, not the crystals, because the water has a lower boiling point. Some of the crystals were exactly the same as before, and some assumed a slightly different formation. They all tasted the same as before, except the alcohol solution, which left no crystals of course. In this case, the alcohol evaporated, not the water, because alcohol has a lower boiling point than water. After the alcohol boiled off, therefore, the water no longer had an alcoholic taste.

Evaporation is a quick and efficient means of separating solvents and solutes. It is used in extracting sugar from cane syrup and in purifying salt. The process, when followed by condensation, is called distillation, as you know, and is used to purify water for special purposes.

HOW TO TELL IF A SOLUTION IS AN ELECTROLYTE

Gather these materials: Six small jars; 2 dry cells; three 6-inch lengths of insulated copper wire and one 4-inch length; a small flashlight bulb; a kitchen knife or penknife; dilute sulfuric acid (H_2SO_4); acetic acid (CH_3COOH); sodium chloride (NaCl); starch ($C_6H_{10}O_5$); magnesium sulfate ($MgSO_4$); and salad oil.

Follow this procedure: Arrange the 6 jars in a row and label each one with the name of one of the chemicals listed above. Fill the first 5 jars halfway with water. Add 1½ teaspoonfuls of sulfuric acid to the jar labeled "sulfuric acid," 1½ teaspoonfuls of acetic acid to the jar labeled "acetic acid," and so forth until you get to the jar labeled "salad oil." Fill that jar, which contains no water, halfway with salad oil.

Using your penknife, remove ½ inch of insulation from both ends of each piece of copper wire. Connect one of the 6-inch lengths of wire to one of the dry cells at the outside terminal. Make the connection by winding the wire 1½ coils around the terminal. Connect the central terminal of the same dry cell to the outside terminal of the second dry cell with the 4-inch length of wire. Connect the second 6-inch length of wire to the central terminal of the second dry cell. You now have this arrangement from left to right: 6-inch wire, dry cell, 4-inch wire, dry cell, 6-inch wire. Wrap one of the loose ends of wire around the threads (screw-type grooves) of the flashlight bulb. Be sure the connection is very tight. In the remaining wire, make an S-shaped bend about 2 inches from one end, so that you can rest it on the edge of a jar. Make a similar S-shaped loop in the free end of the wire connected to the dry cell. Check the diagram.

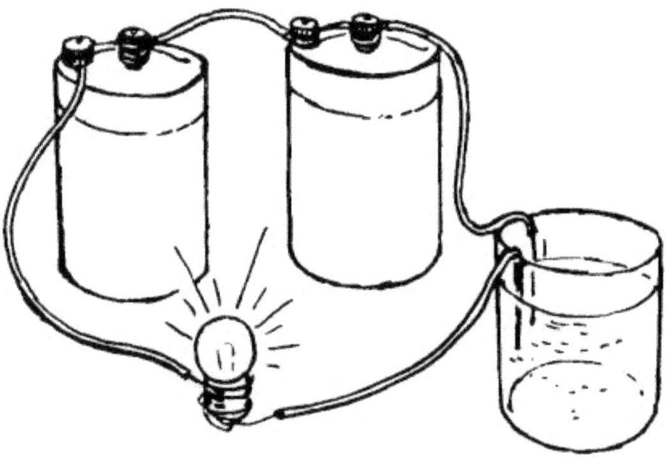

Now put both S-shaped loops over the edge of the jar containing sulfuric acid, so that both wire ends are in the solution. Touch the end of the unconnected wire resting in the sulfuric acid solution to the small knob at the bottom of the bulb. Make a note of what happens to the bulb. Repeat this procedure with each of the five other jars. Wipe off the ends of the wires with a damp cloth every time you substitute a new solution.

Results: When you used the solutions of sulfuric acid, acetic acid, sodium chloride, and magnesium sulfate, the bulb lit up. It did not light up when you used the starch and salad oil.

In the cases where the bulb lit up, the solutions were electrolytes, that is, liquids that allow electrical current to pass through them. Most acid, base, and salt solutions are electrolytes. The four solutions that were electrolytes served to complete the circuit-the continuous path that electricity follows from its source (here, the dry cells) to the appliance (here, the flashlight bulb). In the cases where the bulb did not light up, the liquids were not electrolytes. The starch and salad oil were neither acids, bases, nor salts. Because electricity could not pass through them, they broke the circuit instead of completing it. The electricity, therefore, failed to reach the bulb.

HOW YOU CAN OBSERVE DIFFUSION

Gather these materials: Three small glasses filled with water; 1 crystal of potassium permanganate ($KMnO_4$); 1 crystal of rock salt ($NaCl$); a glass rod; black India ink; an eyedropper.

Follow this procedure: Let the glasses of water stand until the water appears to be perfectly still and motionless. Drop the crystal of potassium permanganate into one, the crystal of salt in the next, and a drop of India ink into the third. Do not stir, touch or move the water in the glasses. Watch them for several minutes and notice what happens. Allow them to stand overnight, and then check the appearance of the three solutions. Using a glass rod, taste a drop of the sodium chloride solution in the second glass.

Results: At first the potassium permanganate crystal made a thin line of color as it fell through the water. Soon the water around the crystal became colored. After standing all night, the crystal dissolved almost completely and the entire glass of water became the same shade of violet.

As you watched the crystal of rock salt fall through the water, there was no visible change because the salt and water both are colorless. However, the rock salt crystal did begin to dissolve almost at once. After standing all night, the entire glass of water tasted salty.

As it fell through the water, the drop of India ink assumed a cloud-like shape, but nevertheless fell to the bottom. After standing all night, the ink colored the entire glassful of water evenly.

This mixing occurred without your touching the solutions. The molecules of water as well as the molecules of the crystals and the ink were constantly in motion, as all molecules are. In moving about, they bumped into each other and rebounded, so that their motion was continuous. Even though the motion was a random one, it resulted eventually in an even distribution throughout the water of the substances you added to it. This is called diffusion. Diffusion occurs in all fluids (liquids and gases) that combine in a purely mechanical way (as opposed to combining chemically, that is, when there is no chemical change in the molecules of the substances involved). Diffusion also occurs when any fluid or solid dissolves in a fluid. Thus diffusion can result in either a suspension or a true solution.

HOW YOU CAN OBSERVE OSMOSIS

Gather these materials: Several fresh, uncooked eggs; a glass tube or drinking straw; a small glass (just the right size to hold an egg, but not large enough to let the egg fall in); a penknife; and a candle.

Follow this procedure: Notice that the two ends of an egg are not exactly alike. One end is more rounded than the other. Choose one egg and decide which end is rounder. Using the point of the sharp edge of your penknife, scrape the eggshell on the rounded end until you can see a thin skin on the inside. There is one thin skin directly attached to the shell and another about ⅛ of an inch beneath it. You cannot help breaking the first skin, but don't break the second one. Now carefully chip off the eggshell until it has a hole slightly smaller than a dime. The contents of the egg will not drop out if you haven't broken the inside skin. If you have, put the egg aside, return it to your mother (she can still use it for cooking), and try again with another egg. Don't be discouraged if you break the inside skin on several eggs. This requires patience and a steady hand. Practice helps, too.

When you have succeeded in this part of the experiment, fill the small glass with water, and set the egg on the rim so that the open hole is beneath the surface of the water. Take your penknife again, and in the pointed end of the egg, make a very small hole, deeper than the other one. Make this hole go right into the egg white. This hole will be easier to make because you don't have to worry about breaking the skin. Put one end of the glass tube or drinking straw into the egg white through this second hole. Make the opening around the tube airtight by sealing the space between the eggshell and the tube with candle wax. You can do this by lighting a candle and, when the wax begins to melt, tipping the candle over so that the wax falls' on the area you want sealed. Now let the egg, glass, and tube stand undisturbed overnight. In the morning, break the egg and examine the egg white.

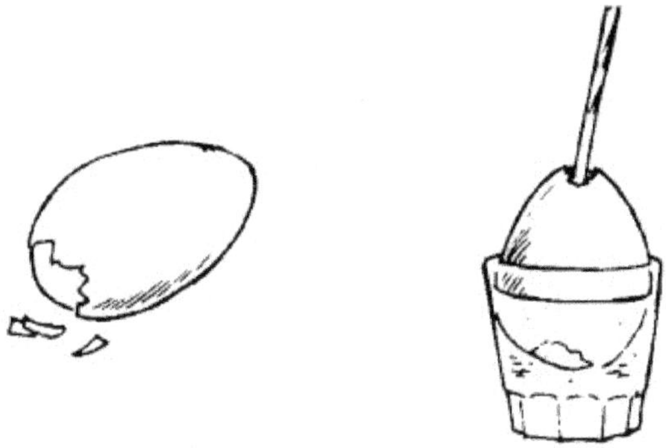

Results: By morning the level of the fluid in the tube was above the surface of the eggshell. The water in the glass was at a lower level than it was originally. When you examined the egg white it was much thinner than ordinary uncooked egg white. What actually happened?

Any living skin tissue which is very, very thin is called a *membrane*. Like all living things, membranes are made of cells, the basic structural unit of plants and animals. Membranes seem to be strong and solid, but if you looked at one under a microscope, you would see that the walls of the cells are porous. Because of these pores, *osmosis* can take place. Osmosis is the process by which molecules pass through the pores in the cell walls of a membrane. Osmosis, in other words, is diffusion through a membrane.

In the experiment with the egg, water molecules from the glass of water passed through the thin skin of the egg and pushed the egg white up into the tube. Actually, while the water molecules passed up into the egg, some of the egg white molecules also passed down into the water. But because molecules move faster from a thin liquid, like water, to a thicker one, like egg white, there was not yet enough egg white in the water to be clearly visible.

The process of osmosis is very important in our lives because all the air we breathe, the food we eat, and the wastes our bodies must remove pass through the cell membranes in this manner.

ANOTHER WAY OF OBSERVING OSMOSIS

Gather these materials: Two thistle tubes or small glass funnels; 2-pint jars; 2 upright stands and clamps; 3 test tubes; an alcohol burner; some transparent cellulose wrapping paper; 2 Tubber bands; sucrose ($C_{12}H_{22}O_{11}$); crystals of copper sulfate ($CuSO_4$); and some Benedict's solution.

Follow this procedure: 1. First you will have to learn how to test for the presence of sugar because you will need to know this later in the experiment. Label the jars 1 and 2. Fill jar No. 1 halfway with warm water. Dissolve 3 teaspoonfuls of sugar in the water. Now pour a little of the sugar solution into a test tube and add 3 teaspoonfuls of Benedict's solution. Heat the test tube over the alcohol burner until the liquid boils. Now place 2 teaspoonfuls of plain water in a fresh test tube and add an equal amount of Benedict's solution. Heat the test tube over the alcohol burner until the liquid boils.

Results: When you boiled the sugar solution with Benedict's solution added, it turned brick red. The color of the plain water with Benedict's solution added stayed the same when you boiled it. Benedict's solution provides a chemical test for sugar. When you add it to a solution containing sugar and boil the two together, the liquid turns brick red. This only happens if the solution contains sugar.

2. Fill one of the thistle tubes with plain water. Cover the mouth with the cellulose wrapping paper and hold it firm with a rubber band. Invert the thistle tube and place it in the jar of sugar solution (jar No.1). With the clamp, attach the thistle tube to the upright stand at such a height that the paper is well below the surface of the sugar solution. (The diagram shows you how to fix your apparatus.) Allow this to stand at least for several hours or preferably overnight.

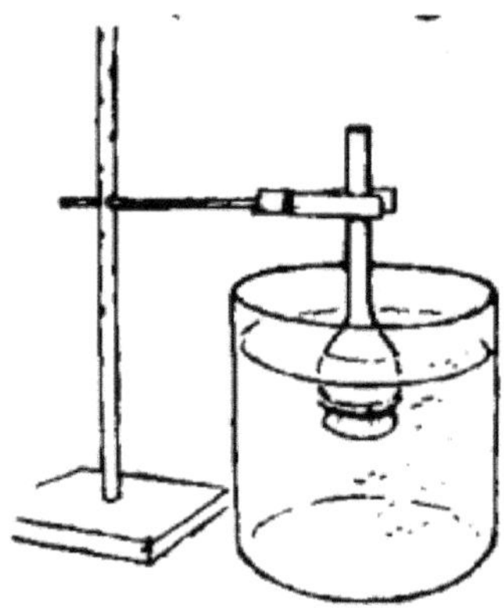

Fill jar No.2 with plain water. Put! cup of warm water in the other thistle tube and add 3 teaspoonfuls of copper sulfate to it. Then cover the mouth of the thistle tube with wrapping paper, and invert the thistle tube in the jar of plain water, as you did before. Hold it in the right place with the clamp. Allow this to stand overnight also.

Results: Since plain water is colorless and copper sulfate is blue, you had no difficulty observing what happened in jar No.2. The blue solution in the thistle tube was less blue, whereas the formerly colorless water in the jar turned blueish. This means that molecules of copper sulfate got into the water in the jar and vice versa.

Since the sugar solution in jar No. 1 and the plain water in the thistle tube are both colorless, you can't see any changes with your eyes. But you can tell if there were any by testing the plain water for sugar. Take 2 teaspoonfuls of the liquid from the thistle tube and pour it into a fresh test tube. Add 2 teaspoonfuls of Benedict's solution. Heat the test tube over the alcohol burner until the liquid boils. Notice that the color turns brick red, proving that the "plain water" now contains sugar. If you test the sugar solution in the jar, too, you will find that it does not turn quite such a deep brick red, showing that it lost some sugar. Sugar molecules from the jar got into the thistle tube and water molecules from the thistle tube got into the jar.

You have just proved again that molecules pass back and forth through membranes. In this case, the wrapping paper acted as a membrane.

THE CHEMISTRY OF CRYSTALS

Many substances have a crystalline form, especially salts. A *crystal* is a solid piece of matter composed of many atoms arranged in specific patterns. Each crystalline substance has its own crystal pattern, just as each person has his own fingerprints and no one else's. Crystals of any given chemical may vary in size, but the arrangement of the atoms within the crystals does not vary. When many crystals of a substance accumulate, the same pattern repeats itself over and over, with only slight variations depending on the size and purity of the crystal. Snowflakes, which are melting ice crystals, have a 6-sided, or hexagonal pattern. The smaller crystals that band together to make up a large snowflake are all 6-sided figures, too.

Sometimes crystals include molecules of water along with their own atoms. The water molecules affect the appearance of the crystal but not its chemical characteristics. In its ordinary crystalline form, copper sulfate contains water molecules and has a lovely blue color. When dissolved in a liquid, these crystals form a solution of the same blue color. If the blue crystalline form is heated, however, or crushed into a powder, it loses the water molecules and becomes white. Nevertheless, it still has all of the same chemical properties it had before.

Water molecules, when included in crystals, make up *water of crystallization*, also called *water of hydration*. (All crystals are not capable of including water molecules.) When crystals lose water of crystallization through evaporation, the process is called *efflorescence*. When crystals absorb water from the air, the process is called *deliquescence*. The following experiments will show you the effects of efflorescence and deliquescence.

HOW YOU CAN DETECT WATER OF HYDRATION

Gather these materials: Copper sulfate crystals ($CUSO_4$); sodium carbonate crystals (Na_2CO_3); 2 test tubes; an alcohol burner; a few drops of water; and paper and pencil.

Follow this procedure: Write down a description of the appearance of each of the two types of crystal. Put a small quantity of each into separate test tubes. Heat them one at a time for several minutes over the alcohol burner. At the end of this time, write a description of each substance and compare it with the original description. Allow the test tubes to cool. Put 1 or 2 drops of water in each tube. Note and record the result.

Results: The crystals became powdery and/or lost their color when you heated them. They regained their original color and form when you later added water.

When crystals containing water of hydration are heated, the water molecules evaporate, and the substance changes in appearance. It becomes powdery and if it was colored, it loses its color. Since it becomes powdery, it is apparent that water of hydration helps to hold the atoms of crystals in a particular pattern. When the water is replaced, the crystals regain their original color and form.

HOW YOU CAN DISCOVER AND USE EFFLORESCENCE AND DELIQUESCENCE

Gather these materials: A kitchen scale delicate enough to record the weight of 3 teaspoonfuls of a chemical salt; crystalline sodium carbonate (Na_2CO_3);
solid pellets of sodium hydroxide (NaOH); filter paper; and paper and pencil.

Follow this procedure: Write a description of the appearance of each substance. Put 3 teaspoonfuls of each chemical on 2 different pieces of clean filter paper and weigh each paper. CAUTION: Do not let the sodium hydroxide touch your skin. If it does, wash it immediately with lots of cool water. Record the weights of each paper. Now spread the substances out, each on its own filter paper, and let them stand overnight. Weigh them in the morning. Record the changes.

Results: The sodium hydroxide gained weight and the sodium carbonate lost weight. There was also a distinct change in the appearance of both chemicals. Why did these changes occur?

The sodium carbonate lost weight because it lost its water of hydration through evaporation.

The sodium hydroxide gained weight because it absorbed water from the air. How do you think this information could be put to practical use? Remember, loss of water is efflorescence and gain of water is deliquescence.

There are many drugs, textiles, commercial chemicals, even substances in the basements of homes and summer cottages that are affected by the presence of moisture in the air. You have probably seen clothing become mildewed and medicines become spoiled by too much or too little moisture. This is where knowledge of efflorescence and deliquescence can be put to use. Drug manufacturers, for example, can keep moisture in the air of their stock rooms by exposing efflorescent chemicals. In a summer home, your parents can prevent the furniture and clothing from being spoiled by dampness by exposing deliquescent chemicals. One deliquescent chemical is paraformaldehyde (CH2O2). Itis a big word but it can save a lot of money.

HOW YOU CAN GROW CRYSTAL GARDEN

Gather these materials: Sodium silicate (Na_2SiO_3); cobalt chloride ($CoCI_2$); copper sulfate ($CuSo_4$); manganous sulfate ($MnSO_4$); lead nitrate ($Pb(NO_3)_2$); ferrous sulfate ($FeSO_4$); a glass pie pan or shallow bowl; an 8-inch length of rubber tubing; a beaker; and water. If you should have difficulty in getting any of these chemicals, ask your druggist for any metallic salts that form colored crystals.

Follow this procedure: In the shallow pan, mix 1 cup of sodium silicate with 4 cups of water.

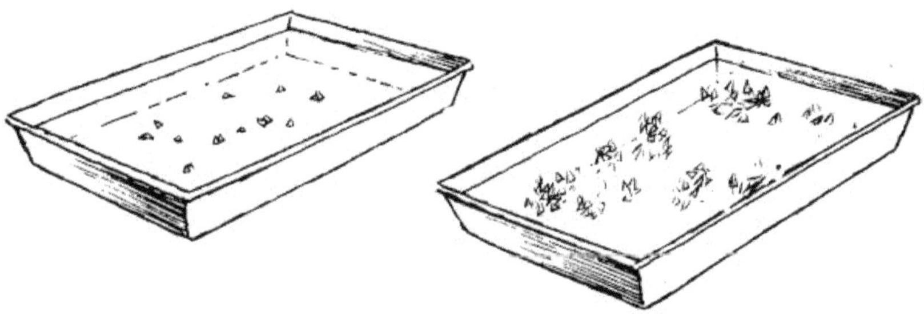

The water should be slightly warmer than room temperature. Stir until you are sure the water and sodium silicate have thoroughly mixed. Place one or two of each type of crystal in the solution in no particular pattern, but be sure to allow enough space between the crystals to give them room to grow. Once you have added the crystals, do not disturb the pan. When the crystals have stopped growing, siphon off the sodium silicate solution, and replace it with clear water. This will preserve your crystal garden.

Results: As the solution cooled, the colors blended and produced a surprisingly beautiful effect.

In this crystal garden, all the crystals are basically sodium silicate. Pure sodium silicate crystals are colorless, but in the areas around the metallic salts, the sodium silicate incorporated some of the metal molecules. These produced much of the color effect. The greater the number of facets (flat faces) on each crystal, the more beautiful is the crystal garden. The more facets there are, the more angles there are, and these reflect and refract (bend) the light. Refraction causes the light to disperse, or break up into many beautiful colors.

HOW TO GROW GIANT CRYSTALS

Gather these materials: Rock candy which is crystallized sugar ($Cl12H22O11$); rock salt ($NaCl$); copper sulfate ($CuSO4$); cobalt chloride ($CoCl2$): ferrous sulfate ($FeSO4$); 5 splints or pencils; 5 drinking glasses; at least 30 inches of string; a kettle or small pot; and a tray large enough to hold the 5 glasses. Obtain your mother's permission to use the stove.

Follow this procedure: Pour 6 glasses of water into the kettle. The extra glassful will compensate for evaporation by boiling. Put the kettle on the stove and allow the water to boil. While you are waiting, label each glass with the name of one of the chemicals listed above. Then cut the string into 5 lengths, each ¾ of an inch shorter than the drinking glasses. To one end of each string, tie one small crystal of the salts listed above. Tie the other end of each string around the middle of a splint. Place the splints across the tops of the glasses so that the crystals are suspended about! inch from the bottoms of the glasses. Put the glasses aside until later. When the water has boiled, remove the splints and fill each glass halfway. Add 1 teaspoonful of rock candy to the first glass and stir. Add 1 teaspoonful of rock salt to the second glass and stir. In the same fashion, add 1 teaspoonful of the remaining crystals to the remaining glasses of boiled water. Then start all over again in the same order and repeat the process once, twice, or as often as necessary until the solution is saturated. Now fill each glass with water that is still boiling, and repeat the whole procedure again, until each glass contains a supersaturated solution.

Slowly lower each string into the glass that contains a solution of the same substance as the crystal tied on the end. Let the splint rest on the rim of the glass. Place all 5 glasses on the tray and move them to a place where no one will disturb them. Allow them to cool. When they are as cool as the room they are in, move them to a slightly cooler place.

Move the whole tray at once and do it gently, so that the contents of each glass remain undisturbed. After an hour, move them to a still cooler place, perhaps the refrigerator. Lowering the temperature gradually and moving the tray without disturbing the contents of the glasses is extremely important for the success of this experiment. Once the solutions have cooled to about 40° F., let them stand for several days.

Results: There was a point at which each solution became saturated, although some reached this point sooner than others. As the solutions cooled, other crystals, similar to the one on the string, began to form in clusters around it. If you were lucky, you found one large crystal growing steadily larger. No matter how many crystals formed, all the crystals of each chemical were the same shape and had the same general appearance regardless of size. Crystals tied on the string were seed crystals. They provided surfaces for the others to grow around. When the solutions cooled, some of the solutes separated out in crystalline patterns, characteristic of the particular solute.

This experiment can be very time-consuming because giant crystals do not grow readily. They tend to break off into small crystals. Therefore, you must repeat the experiment over and over before obtaining a satisfactory result. But you will find it well worth the time and patience required. Scientists are among the most patient people on earth.

THE CHEMISTRY OF FIRE

For mankind, the discovery of fire and how to use it was probably the single most important event that ever happened. In the beginning man, like his animal companions on earth, was a victim of his environment. He had no protection from the cold weather or from the severe rain and snowstorms that geologists know must have occurred in periods before the beginning of history. Primitive men were hunters. They had to wander about in search of animals for food, so they couldn't settle down and live in one place. And of course, they had to go out and hunt every day because they couldn't very well stock up on meat without an icebox. While the hunter was away from the cave he called home, he worried about wild animals attacking his family back at the cave. At night not everyone could sleep, because most predatory animals are night dwellers, and someone in the family had to stay awake to protect the others.

Scientists think that early men may have discovered fire in one of two ways. They may have seen fire resulting from volcanic eruptions.

Eruptions are natural explosions that take place inside mountains. They eject flames and huge quantities of hot gases and ashes. Or early men may have seen forest fires caused by lightning. However the discovery of fire came about, men soon learned to use it and became very dependent on it.

Living in a cave with a fire at its entrance, the family was suddenly safe from wild animals, because they are afraid of fire and won't approach it. As long as the fire was burning, therefore, everyone could sleep. The fire provided warmth, too, and a stove for cooking meat.

You are certainly aware of the fascination of a flame. Hardly anyone can sit near a campfire or before an open fireplace without watching the fire intently. But just what is a flame? The only way to discover what it really is is to examine chemically how it is produced.

HOW YOU CAN DISCOVER WHAT A FLAME IS

Gather these materials: A wooden match; a wax taper; a small candle; a cigarette lighter; a piece of paper; and 4 clean cool saucers from the kitchen. (Obtain your mother's permission to use the saucers.)

Follow this procedure: Strike the match. Hold the yellow part of the flame close under the bottom of one of the saucers. Notice what happens. Blow the match out and examine the underside of the saucer for moisture. Light the wax taper. Hold the yellow part of the flame close to the underside of the next saucer. Blowout the taper and examine the saucer. Follow the same procedure, using the candle and the cigarette lighter.

Results: Whenever the yellow part of a flame came in contact with a cool dish, a black substance was deposited. This substance is carbon. When carbon burns incompletely, which is usually the case, it glows with a yellow color. A flame is made of tiny particles of very hot carbon. When they cool quickly, as they did on striking the cool dish, they were deposited there as black carbon.

When they cool more slowly, as above an open flame, they join with atoms of oxygen from the air and become carbon dioxide (CO_2), a colorless invisible gas. You found the bottom of the saucers damp. Every flame gives off water vapor also. This is because the fuel contains hydrogen, which combines with oxygen in the air to form water vapor. Wherever there is a fire then, there is carbon in the flame, and there are two by-products-carbon dioxide and water vapor.

Anything that will burn up can be called *fuel,* and all fuels have certain chemical characteristics in common. Most of them contain carbon, hydrogen, or both. They are usually *organic hydrocarbons.* The word "organic" means that the substance was once alive. Wood, for example, was once a tree. Coal comes from whole forests that were alive many eons ago. Charcoal also comes from wood, but in a different way. Oil, kerosene, benzine, even wax, all come from petroleum, which in turn comes from small drops of oil in the bodies of long-dead *diatoms*, microscopic creatures (hat live in water. The word "hydrocarbon" means a substance that contains hydrogen and carbon.

Burning is *combustion*, and combustion is a type of *oxidation*. Oxidation means becoming combined chemically with oxygen. Oxidation is a type of chemical reaction called *exothermic*, meaning that the reaction gives off heat energy. *Exo-* is a prefix meaning "out." The root, *thermic*, comes from a Greek word meaning "heat." Some chemical reactions do not give out heat but instead require that it be added. These are called *endothermic* reactions. *Endo-* is a prefix meaning "in."

Now let us see the chemical equations for the oxidation of carbon and hydrogen:

$C + O2$ $CO2$ (This reaction occurs when there is enough oxygen for the formation of carbon dioxide.)

$2C + O_2$ $2CO$ (This reaction occurs when there is only enough oxygen for the formation of carbon monoxide, a poisonous gas.)

$2H_2 + O_2$ $2H_2O$ These reactions give off the energy you feel and see as *heat* and *light*.

WHAT ARE THE DIFFERENT PARTS OF A FLAME?

Gather these materials: A rather large plumber's candle; an alcohol burner; and a 10-inch piece of glass tubing drawn out to a fine nozzle at one end. Obtain your mother's permission to use the gas stove. If your family doesn't have a gas stove, you will have to omit the parts of the experiment that require it.

Follow this procedure: Light the candle, the alcohol burner, and the gas stove. Compare the three flames. Note any differences that you see. Now place the end of the glass tubing with the larger opening in the center of the candle flame, right next to the wick. After a few seconds, try to light the gas escaping from the nozzle end of the tube. Record the result. Follow the same procedure with the alcohol flame and then the gas flame. In each case, be sure to put the tube in the center of the flame. Compare all the results.

Results: No two of the flames looked exactly alike, but they all had some things in common. The candle flame was mostly yellow, but the central portion was blue. The alcohol flame was very blue (if the wick of your burner was clean) but it, too, had a central, brighter blue cone. The gas flame (if the stove was in good working order) was blue also, but its central cone was even more distinct. These differences were because you were burning different fuels. However, if you remember the definition of a fuel, you know that they are usually hydrocarbons and produce carbon dioxide (and/or carbon monoxide) and water vapor when burning. The central cones form as a result of an incomplete supply of oxygen. The fuel burns best at its outer edges, where it comes in contact with air-that is where it gets the oxygen it needs. In the center of the flame, the gases are incompletely burned or hardly burned at all. That is why you could lead them off through the glass tube and burn them again at the nozzle end.

The hottest part of any flame is directly above the inner cone. Can you guess why? When the flame of a hydrocarbon is yellow, or when the inner cone is very large in comparison with the outer one, the fuel is not being completely burned. This means waste, and waste is expensive. This would be a good time to check your gas stove and ask your parents to have it fixed if it is burning yellow.

HOW YOU CAN SHOW THAT FIRES NEED AIR

Gather these materials: Two small glasses; 2 large glasses; 2 glass chimneys; 6 birthday candles; and 9 corks.

Follow this procedure: On a fireproof portion of your laboratory table, arrange the candles so that they are about 8 inches apart. Fasten them to the table with their own wax, so they won't fall over during the experiment. Arrange the pieces of glassware as follows: a small glass behind each of the first two candles, a large glass behind each of the next two candles, and a glass chimney behind each of the last two candles. Put three corks near the second, fourth, and sixth candles. Light candle No. 1. Cover it with the small glass, inverted. Note the behavior of the flame. Light candle No.2. Arrange the corks in a triangle around its base and place the glass on the corks. Watch the flame and see how it behaves. Repeat this procedure with the remaining candles and the glassware behind them. Each time observe the behavior of the flames, and at the end, compare your observations.

Results: In the glasses that didn't rest on corks, the flames went out rather quickly. The large glass, however, allowed the flame to burn longer than the small one did. In the glasses resting on corks, it is possible that the flames didn't go out at all if the corks were very large. In the glass chimneys, neither flame went out, but the flame inside the chimney resting on corks was stronger and brighter.

The union of oxygen from the air with a burning fuel produces flame. Since fire results from oxidation, it obviously cannot occur without oxygen. No air could enter the glasses covering candles Nos. 1 and 3. They went out as soon as they used up the oxygen that was already in the air inside the glasses. The glass over candle No. 3 was larger and contained more air, to begin with, so candle No. 3 burned a little longer. A little air entered the glasses covering candles Nos. 2 and 4 through the opening made by the corks between the glasses and the table. Therefore, they continued to burn. The candles under the glass chimneys also continued to burn, because air entered from above. Candle No.6, however, burned more strongly, because it had a supply of air both from above and below.

NOTE: experiments marked with an asterisk (*) are potentially dangerous. Parents should decide how much supervision is necessary.

HOW YOU CAN MAKE A FUEL

Gather these materials: An alcohol burner and a "fishtail tip"; an upright stand and clamp; I pyrex test tube; one 8-inch length of glass tubing; a triangular file; a 1-holed stopper; some lumps of coal; a pie pan; paper towels; and a hammer.

Follow this procedure: Place the fishtail tip on the alcohol burner and light it. Rotate the glass tubing in the flame by holding each end, as you learned on page 21. When the flame becomes bright orange and when the glass is soft, pull the ends apart quickly. Allow the glass to cool. CAUTION: Remember that hot glass does not look hot. Don't touch it for a while. When the glass is cool, cut the ends with the triangular file to form two nozzles. Fire-polish both ends.

Place the coal on the pie pan and cover it with paper towels. Using the hammer, smash it into small pieces. Make it almost as fine as powder. Fill the test tube about halfway with the powdered coal. Fit the nozzle into the stopper as shown in the diagram, and according to your safety rules.

Heat the coal over the burner for several minutes, then light the gas coming from the nozzle.

Results: When you heated the coal, it gave over the gases, mainly methane (CH_4) and ethane (C_2H_6), that were trapped in it as it was formed in the earth. This gaseous mixture burned with a characteristic blue flame. The material which remained in the test tube is a form of carbon called coke. If there was any sticky brownish substance there, too, it was a combination of coal tar products, which are the residue of coal burned in this way.

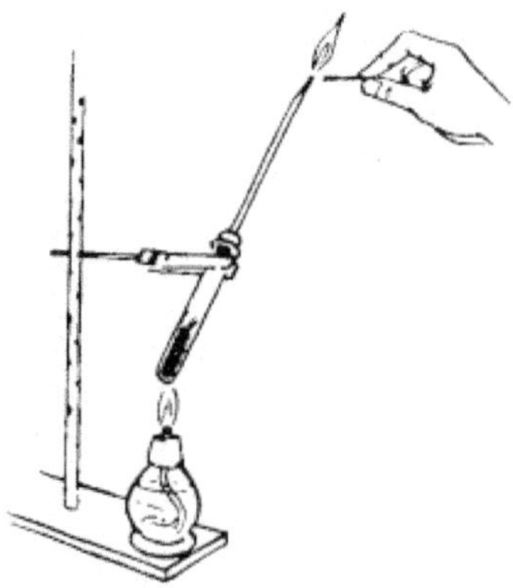

With the energy provided by sunlight, plants build up their own tissues out of minerals and water from the earth and from carbon dioxide from the air. These decayed plant tissues in sunken forests become coal deposits, and the elements which they contained pass into the coal. Coal is basically carbon, and without the additional elements from the plant tissues, it would be pure carbon. When you heated the coal, these other elements were forced out of the tube through the nozzle in the form of a gaseous mixture. This is one of several gaseous mixtures used in gas stoves. When an industrial company manufactures gas like this, it passes steam over the hot coal to make the process more efficient.

The remaining "coal" is also sold as coke.

HOW TO MAKE ANOTHER FUEL

Gather these materials: An upright stand and clamp; an alcohol burner; 2 test tubes; one 1-holed stopper and one 2-holed stopper; 3 wooden splints broken in half (or 6 wooden matches with the "heads" removed); 1 piece of glass tubing bent at a 45-degree angle; 1 piece of glass tubing stretched to form a nozzle; and a test tube rack.

Follow this procedure: Using the upright stand and clamp, arrange one test tube at a 45-degree angle pointing upward. Put the pieces of wood into it. Insert the bent glass tubing into the l-holed rubber stopper, and insert the stopper into the mouth of the test tube. Put the other end of this glass tubing through the 2-holed rubber stopper. Put the 2-holed rubber stopper into the second test tube, and push the glass tubing down to the bottom of the test tube. Put the glass tubing with the nozzle end into the other hole in the 2-holed stopper. Put the second test tube in the rack. Check the diagram to see that your apparatus is set up correctly. Now light the alcohol burner and heat the dry wood. Watch the second test tube. After about 5 minutes of heating, hold a match to the end of the nozzle.

Results: There was no flame inside the test tube containing wood. Since you did not apply flame directly to the wood, it didn't reach its kindling point. Nevertheless, you could see that it was being burned up. The heat was great enough to force certain chemicals out of the wood. These collected in the form of the yellowish liquid in the second test tube. When you brought a match near the nozzle, the gas escaping from the yellow liquid ignited.

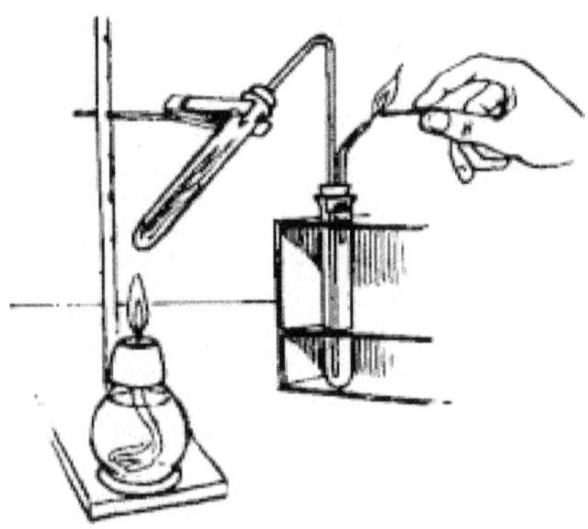

The loss of certain chemicals changed the wood in the test tube into *charcoal,* a commercially valuable fuel. The yellow liquid, driven off from the wood, contains chemicals that are a source of valuable drugs and dyes.

THE CHEMISTRY OF ACIDS, BASES AND SALTS

You must learn a little about the chemical composition and structure of acids and bases. But it will be easier to do this if first we take another look at an old friend, H_2O.

As you know, water is a combination of two kinds of atoms-hydrogen and oxygen. One of the hydrogen atoms in a molecule of water can act independently, while the other one cannot; it always accompanies the oxygen atom. You are used to seeing the formula for water written as H_2O. It can be written correctly in another way, too: H-OH is exactly the same in numerical value. H-OH, however, shows not only how many atoms of hydrogen and oxygen there are in a molecule of water, but also how they are arranged. In other words, it shows the chemical structure as well as the chemical composition of a molecule of water. This is the empirical way of writing the formula for water.

Now let's see what this empirical formula tells us about water. There is no dash between the OH. This means that these two atoms are very tightly bound together and that if the whole water molecule breaks up, these two atoms will still stay together. If they move to another molecule, they will move together as one complete unit. Pairs or groups of molecules bound as tightly as this are called *radicals*. The OH radical is often called the *hydroxyl* radical.

The dash after the first H shows that it is bound to the OH radical, but not as tightly as the O and H in the radical. The first H can be separated from the radical fairly easily. If the molecule of water breaks up, the first H will go off by itself. It might remain separate for a while. Or, in a new molecule, it might join a radical again in a fairly loose union, or it might even join with an O to become part of an OH radical itself. When separated, the two parts of the water molecule act differently, but whenever possible they join each other to become water.

Now how does this relate to acids and bases and the effect they have on one another? An acid is a substance with a hydrogen atom that can be easily pushed out of its molecules. Examples of acids are hydrochloric acid (HCl), sulfuric acid (H2SO4), and carbonic acid (H2CO3). A *base* (the same as an *alkali* for all practical purposes) is a substance with an OH radicals that can easily be pushed out of its molecules. Examples of bases are ammonium hydroxide (NH_4OH), calcium hydroxide ($Ca(OH)_2$)' and potassium hydroxide (KOH).

Salts form when an acid and base react with one another. The salt is a compound consisting of the combination of atoms left over after the free H's have detached themselves from the acid and the free OH's from the base. The detached H's and OH's join to become water. Examples of salts are sodium chloride (NaCI), magnesium sulfate ($MgSO_4$), and copper sulfate ($CuSO_4$).

When a salt is formed, water is also formed.

Let us take as a theoretical example the reaction between the base, calcium hydroxide ($Ca(OH)_2$) and the acid, carbonic acid (H_2CO_3). Calcium hydroxide has two OH radicals and carbonic acid has two H's. When you put this acid and base together, you know that the H's and OH's will detach themselves from the acid and base, respectively, and will combine to form water. You know also that the atoms left over-the Ca, C, and O's-will combine to form a salt. See then if you can figure out the equation for this reaction:

$$H_2CO_3 + Ca(OH)_2 \rightarrow 2H_2O + CaCO_3$$

Naturally, it is very important to be able to tell if a molecule has a free H atom or OH radical to give up, in other words, if it is an acid or a base. Chemists have found certain substances, called *indicators*, which change color when they are close to substances containing free H atoms or OH radicals. In the following experiments, you will learn how to use some of these indicators.

HOW YOU CAN TELL AN ACID FROM ABASE

Gather these materials: Carbonic acid (H2CO3); a solution of sodium chloride (NaCl); a dilute solution of ammonium hydroxide (NH4OH); a dilute solution of sodium hydroxide (NaOH); hypochlorous acid (HClO); magnesium sulfate (MgSO4); boric acid (H3BO3); acetylsalicylic acid (CH3COOC6H4COOH); ethanol (C2HsOH); salad or mineral oil (basically (CH2)16CO2H); sodium bicarbonate (NaHCO3); 11 test tubes; some test tube racks; blue and red litmus paper; and paper and pencil.

Follow this procedure: Set up the test tubes in the racks and label each one with one of the chemical names listed above. Put -t teaspoonful of each chemical into the correct tube. Add enough water to fill the tubes to approximately 1/3 their height. Make a data sheet similar to the one here, and as you proceed, fill in the spaces.

Place small strips of blue litmus paper (a fresh one each time) over the rims of the test tubes one by one. Let one end fall into the liquid in the test tube.

Substance	*Reaction of blue litmus paper*	*Reaction of red litmus paper*
H_2CO_3	turned paper red	none
NaCI		
NH_4OH		
NaOH		
HCIO		
$MgSO_4$		
H_3BO_3		
$CH_3COOC_6H_4COOH$		
C_2H_5OH		
$(CH_2)_{16}CO_2H$		
$NaHCO_3$		

Record the results. Repeat the same procedure with red litmus paper, and record the results. Now fill each test tube to the top with water to dilute the solutions. Test the contents of each tube with both blue and red litmus paper again, and again record all the results.

Results: The carbonic acid, the hypochlorous acid, the boric acid, and the acetylsalicylic acid turned the blue litmus paper to red, but had no effect on the red litmus paper. The sodium hydroxide and the ammonium hydroxide turned the red litmus paper to blue, but had no effect on the blue litmus paper. The sodium chloride, magnesium sulfate, ethanol, salad oil, and sodium bicarbonate had no effect on either the red or blue litmus paper.

Acids turn blue litmus to red but have no effect on red. Bases turn red litmus to blue, but have no effect on blue. You can see that it is often necessary to use both to get a conclusive result. The substances that have no effect on either type of litmus paper are neutral. That means they have neither H atoms nor OH radicals willing to be pushed out of their molecules. These neutral substances, therefore, are neither acids nor bases.

Looking at your record of what happened before and after diluting the solutions, you should be able to draw some conclusions about the effect of dilution on the acidity or alkalinity of a solution.

HOW YOU-CAN NEUTRALIZE AN ACID WITH A BASE

Gather these materials: Acetic acid (CH3COOH); a calcium hydroxide solution (Ca(OH)2); red and blue litmus paper; 2 eye droppers; 1 tablespoon and 1 teaspoon; and 2 small jars that are alike.

Follow this procedure: Put 3 tablespoonfuls of acetic acid and 2 tablespoonfuls of water into one jar. Label the jar "acetic acid." Put one eyedropper and the tablespoon you used next to it. Put 1 teaspoonful of calcium hydroxide solution into the other jar. Put the teaspoon and the other eyedropper next to it. Fill this jar halfway with water. Stir the contents of each jar with its individual spoon. Remember, these spoons must not be used for cooking again.

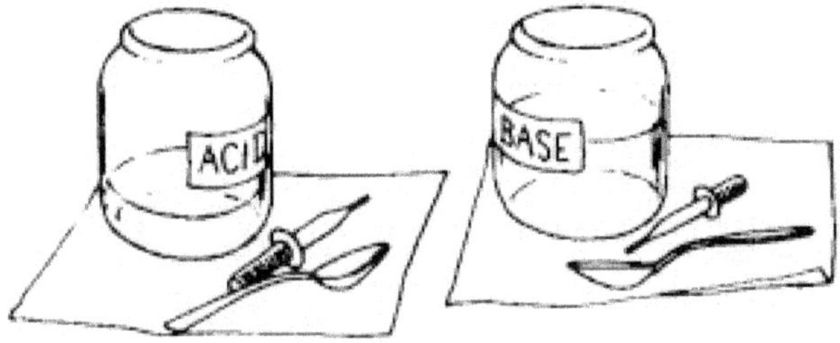

Test the contents of both jars with red and blue litmus paper to see which solution is acid and which solution is alkaline. Place the jar of acid directly in front of you. Place the alkaline solution to the right and slightly behind the acid (unless you are left-handed). Now, with the dropper near the calcium hydroxide, add 3 drops of it to the acetic acid, stir with the spoon near the acetic acid, and test the new solution with blue litmus paper. Repeat this procedure over and over, counting the drops carefully, and noting the amount of change in the litmus paper. When the amount of change begins to become very small use only I drop of alkali at a time. Continue until you reach the point where there is no change at all in the litmus paper.

Results: The change in color of the blue litmus to red became less and less marked as you added more alkali to the acid. This shows that the addition of an alkali was making the solution less and less acid. Finally, you reached a point where the solution had no effect whatsoever on the color of the litmus paper. This was the endpoint, or point of neutralization. Enough alkali had been added so that the solution was definitely no longer acid; it had been neutralized by the alkali. If you had continued to add alkali to the solution after reaching the endpoint, it would slowly have turned into an alkali, and you could have traced its progress by testing it with red litmus paper. The equation for the neutralization in this experiment is:

2CH3COOH + Ca(OH)2 -+ 2H20 + Ca(CH3COO)2

The neutralized liquid is a calcium acetate solution. In a much more elaborate form, the process of gradual neutralization and continuous testing which you performed in this experiment is called titration. Chemists often use titration to tell exactly how many H atoms and/or OH radicals are present in a solution.

This is important in medicine, in the dye and drug industries, and even in preparing the paints for an artist's palette or your house.

THE CHEMISTRY OF PHOTOGRAPHY

You have probably taken many pictures yourself, and posed for many more. Have you ever wondered about the mysterious way that photographs are made? Once you know the natural laws on which photography is based, the process doesn't seem so mysterious. Like all the wonders of our age of modern technology, photography depends on knowing certain natural laws and then putting them to work for our own purposes. Many of the natural laws that we put to work in photography come under the domain of physics, and more especially, optics, the science of light. Optics teaches us how light rays behave and how they are affected when they go through certain kinds of lenses. This knowledge is the basis for the designing of cameras.

The process of developing pictures, however, is essentially a matter of chemistry. The way that light affects and alters certain chemical compounds gives us a means of reproducing and preserving on paper images from real life. In the following section, you will learn about some of the underlying chemical processes that are essential to photography.

HOW YOU CAN SEE THE EFFECT OF SUNLIGHT ON HYDROGEN PEROXIDE

Gather these materials: Two test tubes; 2 small jars; some cellophane tape; some black construction paper; hydrogen peroxide (H_2O_2); 2 upright stands; 2 test tube holders; 2 wooden splints.

Follow this procedure: Cover one test tube completely (except the mouth) with black construction paper. Use the cellophane tape to fasten the construction paper to the test tube. Also cover the outside of one jar. Fill both jars with hydrogen peroxide. Fill the uncovered test tube with hydrogen peroxide, and cover its mouth with your thumb. Invert the tube in the jar that is not paper covered. Push the mouth of the tube about t inch below the surface of the hydrogen peroxide, and then fix the tube in that position with a test tube holder, attached to an upright stand.

Cut out a piece of black construction paper to fit over the surface of the hydrogen peroxide in the paper-covered jar, and make a hole in the middle with a diameter a little larger than the diameter of a test tube. Put this piece of paper over the surface of the hydrogen peroxide. Now fill the covered test tube with hydrogen peroxide and put it, upside down, through the hole in the paper-covered jar, as you did before.

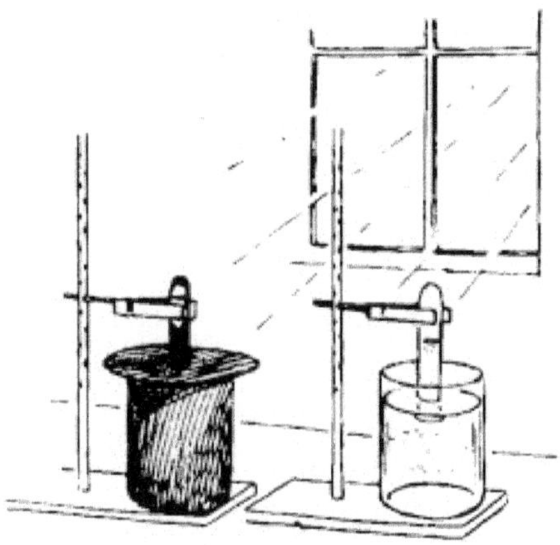

Put all the apparatus in a sunny place and let it stand for 2 hours. At the end of this time, have a glowing splint ready, and holding it in one hand, remove one of the test tubes from its jar with your other hand. In removing it, keep the mouth of the tube covered with your thumb. Take your thumb off the mouth of the tube, and quickly thrust a glowing splint into the test tube. Repeat this procedure with the other test tube.

Results: At the end of 2 hours, gas had collected at the top of the test tubes. There was less gas in the test tube from the paper-covered jar than in the other test tube. When you put a glowing splint into the test tube from the jar exposed to sunlight, the splint burst into a white flame, proving that the gas in that test tube was oxygen. In the other test tube, there was only a slight reaction to the glowing splint.

The light energy of sunlight breaks down the molecules of hydrogen peroxide and detaches one atom of oxygen. The equation for this reaction is:

$$4H_2O_2 \overset{\text{sunlight}}{\quad} 4H_2O + 2O_2$$

Hydrogen peroxide is not the only chemical affected by light. You may have noticed that many drugs and chemicals come in brown or blue glass containers.

These are the ones whose molecules are sensitive to light, and the dark-colored glass prevents most light rays from reaching the contents of the jar.

(Most of the commercial hydrogen peroxide, sold for use as an antiseptic, is a 3 % solution of peroxide in water, but it is called a 10-volume solution. That means that for every measured amount of hydrogen peroxide, the volume of oxygen released will be 10 times as great as the volume of the original hydrogen peroxide solution).

HOW YOU CAN MAKE A BLUEPRINT

Gather these materials: Two shallow pans, preferably glass or plastic; a measuring cup; a tablespoon; ferric oxalate ($Fe_2(C_2O_4)_3$); potassium ferricyanide ($KaFe(CN)_6$); many sheets of white paper; drawing ink; photographic negatives; opaque objects, such as keys, coins or leaves; paper clips; a large black folder or envelope; tracing paper or transparent wrapping paper; and a clean cloth. Remember, the pans cannot be used later for cooking.

Follow this procedure: Add 3 tablespoonfuls of ferric oxalate to 3 cups of water in one of the shallow pans. Dip the sheets of white paper, a few at a time, into the ferric oxalate solution and allow it to dry in a dark place. Ferric oxalate is the chemical for treating the white paper and turning it into blueprint paper. If you are not going to use the blueprint paper immediately, store it in the black envelope when it is dry.

With the drawing ink, make some line drawings on the tracing paper. Attach them to sheets of your blueprint paper with paper clips. Place the opaque objects you gathered on other sheets of blueprint paper. With the paper clips, fasten the photographic negatives to still other sheets of blueprint paper. Put the blueprint papers with the various things attached to them in a sunny place for at least 20 minutes. Expose the transparent paper for a longer time. While you are waiting, add 3 tablespoonfuls of potassium ferricyanide to 3 cups of water in the other shallow pan. This is the developing solution.

At the end of the time of exposure, remove everything from the blueprint papers. Dip the blueprint papers, one after the other, into the developing solution. It will only take a few seconds for the blue color to appear. When it does, remove the papers and carefully wash away the film of chemical from the white areas with a cloth moistened with water. Let your blueprints dry and flatten them under a heavy book before you put them away for good.

Results: The ferric oxalate solution was colorless. When it coated the white paper, the white paper didn't change color. Nevertheless, the white paper became blueprint paper simply because it was coated with ferric oxalate:

The sunlight didn't affect the color of the blueprint paper either, but it did produce a chemical change that you could not see.

The equation for the reaction induced by the sunlight is:

$$Fe_2(C_2O_4)_3 \xrightarrow{\text{sunlight}} 2FeC_2O_4 + 2CO_2$$

You can tell from the equation that the big change was in the placement of the iron (Fe) atoms. In the ferric oxalate, there were two iron atoms in each molecule. However, in the new compound, called ferrous oxalate, there was only one iron atom in each molecule.

When you put the exposed blueprint papers into the developing solution, there was a reaction between the ferrous oxalate and the potassium ferricyanide. This reaction caused the blue color to appear.

Where the blueprint paper remained white, this reaction did not take place, because the drawing ink, the opaque objects and the dark areas of the photographic negatives had prevented exposure of those areas to sunlight. If you had left the ferrous oxalate on the blueprint, it would have eventually reacted with sunlight and ruined the blueprint. Washing the ferrous oxalate away, therefore, made the blueprint permanent.

HOW TO MAKE LIGHT-SENSITIVE PAPER FOR PHOTOGRAPHY

Gather these materials: Two pie pans filled with water; 2 teaspoons; sodium chloride ($NaCl$); silver nitrate ($AgNO_3$); 1 package of index cards; a red light bulb; and some coins, buttons, keys, or leaves. You will need a dark closet in which to work or a room where you can cover the windows and make it dark.

Follow this procedure: Dissolve 1 teaspoonful of sodium chloride in one of the pie pans of water and 1 teaspoonful of silver nitrate in the other. CAUTION: Avoid getting any silver nitrate on your skin. It stains skin dark brown. The stain is very difficult to remove and usually has to wear off. Soak the index cards, several at a time, in the sodium chloride solution. Take them out and let them drain off. They should be wet, but not dripping. Now darken the room. The room needn't be pitch black; you may use a red electric light bulb to see by.

Put the cards in the silver nitrate solution, and allow them to remain in it for 3 to 5 minutes. Then remove the cards and let them dry in a dark place. At this point do not allow the cards to be exposed to any light.

When the cards are dry, place the coins, buttons, keys, or leaves on them. Expose them to strong sunlight or light from a bright fluorescent desk lamp for about 5 minutes. Remove the opaque objects.

Results: The objects left white images on the cards. Those parts of the cards that were uncovered were dark gray or black. Since you did not "fix" the cards, the images will eventually disappear.

The white film that appeared on the cards when you took them out of the silver nitrate solution was the substance that made the cards sensitive to light. The white film, which was so thin you may not have actually seen it, was silver chloride, a compound that resulted from the reaction between the sodium chloride and the silver nitrate. The equation for the reaction is:

$$NaCI + AgNO_3 \quad {}^{\text{sunlight}} \quad NaNO_3 + AgCl$$

The light energy from the sun or the desk lamp separated the silver from the film of silver chloride. This left a dark coating of pure silver on those areas of the cards that were exposed to the light. The other areas were unaffected because the light could not pass through the opaque objects. The white film of silver chloride still covered those areas when you removed the objects. Without "fixing" though, the light will soon affect that silver chloride, too. The white images will then become dark like the rest of the cards. Keep them in a dark place or enclosed in a black envelope.

Don't make any images on this batch, though. Just soak some index cards in a sodium chloride solution, then in a silver nitrate solution, let them dry in a dark place, and store them in a black envelope.

HOW TO MAKE YOUR OWN PHOTOGRAPHIC PLATES

Gather these materials: Eight or 10 small pieces of glass, measuring 3" x 5" or 4" x 4"; 1 package of unflavored gelatin; silver bromide (AgBr); an alcohol burner; a small pot; a red light bulb; black construction paper; paper clips; a detergent; paper towels; aluminum foil; bookends; an eyedropper; a cup; and a glass rod. For part of this experiment, you will need the same dark room you used for the preceding experiment. (Get your mother's permission to use the stove.)

Follow this procedure: Wash the pieces of glass with a detergent, and allow them to dry by standing them on edge on the paper towels. You will have to lean them lightly against the book ends. From this point on, don't touch the glass surfaces with your fingers. Fingerprints are oily and will spoil the photographic plates. Dissolve t of the package of gelatin in t cup of water. Put 1 cup of water into the pot and bring it to a boil on the stove. Add the dissolved gelatin and continue to boil for I minute. Replace the bulb in the area you are using with the red bulb.

Wait a few minutes until your eyes become accustomed to the darkness. Have your eyedropper, glass rod, and silver bromide ready. While the gelatin in the pot is still warm enough to flow like a liquid, dissolve 2 teaspoonfuls of silver bromide in it and stir. Hold one of the glass plates between your fingers by the edges to prevent any finger marks. Carefully cover the upper surface with gelatin by distributing it with the eyedropper and then tipping the plate in different directions until one whole surface is evenly covered. Put this plate aside to dry on the aluminum foil, gelatin side up. Repeat this procedure with all the glass plates.

Take one of your pieces of black construction paper and fold it in half. When a gelatin plate is completely solid and dry, place it between the folded halves. Fold the paper loosely around the plate on the three open sides, so that the plate is completely sealed. Secure these folds with paper clips. Do the same with all the gelatin-covered plates. Do not squeeze or press the plates after enclosing them in the paper or you will disturb the gelatin coating. Stack them loosely, side by side and on edge, between the book ends. You will need these plates, which are now covered by a light-sensitive, gelatinous film, for the next experiment.

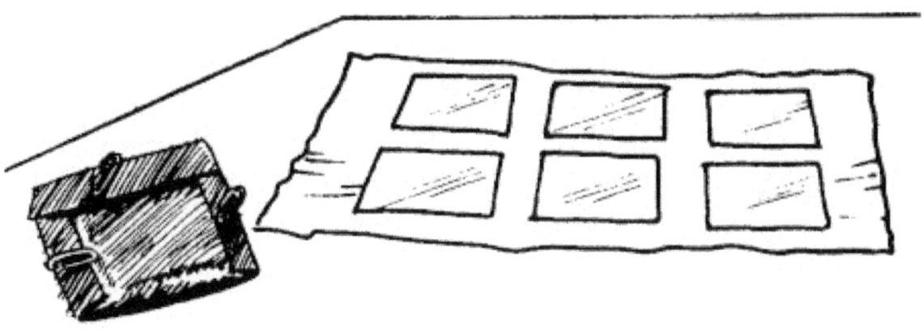

Results: The gelatin became a thick paste in the cool water. When you added it to the boiling water, it dissolved completely. When you dissolved the silver bromide in the gelatin solution, the color of the solution may have changed, but because you worked without light (except from the red bulb), it became no darker than a pale amber. The reason for drying the gelatin-covered plates on the aluminum foil is that aluminum does not absorb water. If you had used paper towels, they would have absorbed some of the water and silver bromide from the gelatin solution and would have spoiled the plates. By folding the open edges of the black paper, you prevented light from getting at the plates and spoiling them.

HOW TO MAKE A NEGATIVE

Gather these materials: Pyrogallic acid ($C_6H_3(OH)3$) or hydroquinone ($C_6H_4(OH)_2$); sodium thiosulfate ($Na_2S_2O_3$); black construction paper; a flashlight with a bright white beam; an upright stand and clamp; the photographic plates you made in the preceding experiments; 4 shallow glass pie plates; a watch or clock; 2 glass stirring rods; bookends; and paper towels. You will have to do most of this experiment in your darkroom, so be sure that the red light bulb is in place.

Follow this procedure: In daylight, arrange your workspace as follows. Attach the flashlight to the upright stand with the clamp. The flashlight should be in a vertical position and about 12inches above the surface you are working on. The bulb should face downward. If the flashlight is too heavy for the clamp, attach it to the stand with cellophane tape or masking tape. Then, starting from the left, stack your photographic plates on the edge next to the upright stand. Use bookends to support them. Have your watch or clock where you can see it easily because you will have to time some of the later procedures in this experiment. Next, line up the 4 pie plates and number them. This may seem unnecessary, but you will find it difficult at first to do things quickly and correctly while working in the dark. It is only sensible, therefore, to have everything marked to lessen the possibility of making mistakes. Now cover your working area with paper towels. In the light, make several stencil designs on the black paper and cut them out. You can easily do this by folding the paper into quarters, then into eighths, and then cutting irregular pieces from each of the folded edges. Now you are ready for the "dark" work. Put out the lights, cover the windows with dark cloth or paper, and proceed with only the red bulb lit.

Fill each pie plate t full of cold water. To plate No. I add 2 teaspoonfuls of pyrogallic acid or hydroquinone. Don't put anything into the water in pie plate No.2. In pie plate No.3 put 2 teaspoonfuls of sodium thiosulfate. Don't put anything in the water in pie plate No.4. Open one of the black envelopes and remove the gelatin-filmed plate. Place it, gelatin side up, on a paper towel directly under the flashlight. Cover the gelatin plate with one of the stencils.

Light the flashlight and watch the clock for 2 minutes. Do not touch or move the plate during these 2 minutes. At the end of this time put out the flashlight and remove the stencil. Place the gelatin-filmed plate in pie plate No.1, which contains the developing solution. Be sure that the solution covers the glass plate completely. Leave the plate in the solution for 2 minutes. Remove it and rinse it in pie plate No.2, then quickly put it into pie plate No.3, which contains the fixative. After 2 minutes rinse it in pie plate No.4, and finally stand it on edge on the paper towels to dry. Use the bookends to support it.

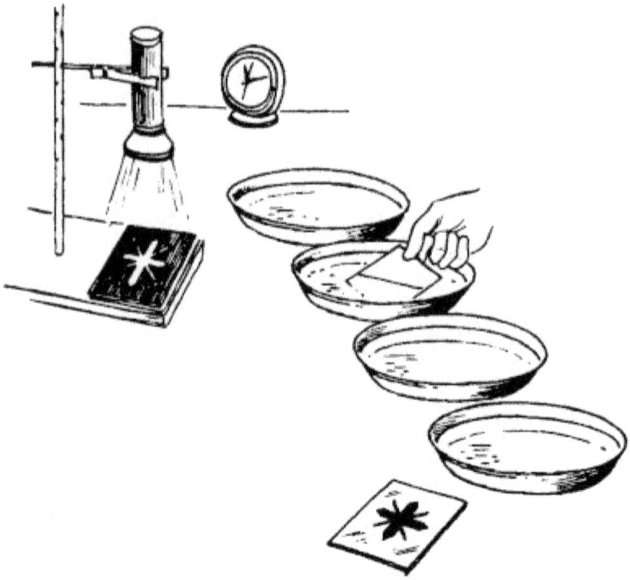

Repeat this procedure with each of the photographic plates. You may find that varying time intervals and different thicknesses of the gelatin coating produce more or less successful results. You will want to experiment a bit until you find the best time exposure for the plates you have made.

Results: When you covered the gelatin-coated surfaces of the photographic plates with the black paper stencils and exposed them to the light from the flashlight, the areas of gelatin not covered by black paper became black themselves. This was because of the effect of light on the silver bromide in the gelatinous coating. It separated the silver from the silver bromide; the dark areas that appeared consisted of pure dark silver, which is insoluble. When you put the photog~aphic plates in t? e pyrogallic acid (the developing solution), the exposed grams of silver bromide were changed to metallic silver, or a silver salt that would not wash away. The sodium thiosulfate (the fixative) in pie plate No.3 *stopped* the action of the developer on the silver bromide. Of course, this is why it is called a fixative. The plate is now a *negative.* The term "negative': indicates that the result is the opposite of the process that caused it. In other words, the plate became dark where it was exposed to light. It is not necessary to store the negatives in a dark place or a black envelope, but be careful not to scratch the surfaces. Save them to use in the next experiment.

HOW TO PRINT A PICTURE FROM ft NEGATIVE, OR MAKING A POSITIVE

Gather these materials: A red light bulb; the light-sensitive paper; an upright stand and clamp; a flashlight attached to the clamp as in the preceding experiment; 4 glass pie plates containing the same liquids as in the preceding experiment, that is, No.1, a pyrogallic acid or hydroquinone solution, No.2, plain water, No.3, a sodium thiosulfate solution, and No.4, plain water; the negatives you made in the preceding experiment; paper towels; and a watch or clock.

Follow this procedure: Set up the apparatus in your darkroom exactly as in the preceding experiment. Work under the red bulb. Take a piece of light-sensitive paper and put one of the negatives you made in the last experiment over it. Arrange other pairs of negatives and. pieces of light-sensitive paper, putting the negatives on top. Place one of the pairs of light-sensitive paper and negative beneath the flashlight. Be sure to keep the gelatin side of the negative up and make no fingerprints on its surface. Turn on the flashlight and allow the pair to stand undisturbed for 3 minutes. Now turn off the light. Put the paper only into each pie plate in turn and time it, as you did in the preceding experiment. You may find that you will have to strengthen your solutions or prolong your time intervals to get the best results. This experimentation with your own equipment to find the very best arrangement is much of the fun of working in a laboratory.

Results: The design on the negative was transferred to the light-sensitive paper, except that the dark areas on the negative came out as light areas on the light-sensitive paper. When you put the negative over the light-sensitive paper and exposed the pair to light, the light reached the light-sensitive paper only through the light parts of the negative. The light-sensitive paper was covered with a film of silver chloride. The exposure to light caused the silver to separate from the silver chloride in the exposed areas, and since the silver is dark, those areas became dark. The solutions that you later dipped the paper into caused the remaining silver chloride to dissolve and transformed the pure silver into an insoluble silver salt that won't wash away.

Many years ago, a Frenchman named Louis Daguerre discovered how to do just what you have done, but instead of paper, he used pieces of silver. Later photographers made tintypes, which were simply Daguerrotypes made on tin plates instead of silver ones.

THE CHEMISTRY OF EVERYDAY THINGS

There is an old saying to the effect that a foolish person wonders only about strange and unusual things but that a wise person wonders about the common, everyday things. Do you ever stop to think about the thousands of things we use every day that are made possible through chemistry? We have gotten so used to most of these things, like rayon and nylon, soap and plastics, that we take them for granted and never stop to think about what they are made of or how they are made. In the following section, you will see for yourself how some of the things you use every day are made.

HOW TO MAKE RAYON THREAD

Gather these materials: Concentrated ammonium hydroxide (NH_4OH); copper sulfate crystals ($CuSO_4$); dilute sulfuric acid (H_2SO_4); a glass stirring rod; a tablespoon; a glass funnel; an eyedropper; filter paper; and 5-pint jars.

Follow this procedure: Fill one of the jars! full of water. Add copper sulfate crystals. Stir the solution and keep adding copper sulfate until no more will dissolve. Pour the liquid off into another jar. With the eyedropper, add concentrated ammonium hydroxide, drop by drop, to the copper sulfate solution until a light blue color appears. Hold the glass rod in your other hand and keep stirring the solution all the time.

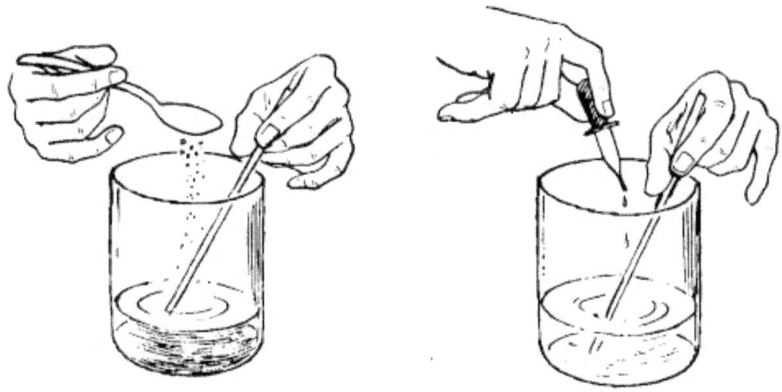

If the solution becomes dark blue, you will have to start all over again. When the ammonium hydroxide ceases to make the solution turn any lighter, pour the liquid through a funnel lined with filter paper into the third jar. Now put the filter paper and everything caught in it into the fourth jar. Add just enough concentrated ammonium hydroxide to dissolve the filter paper. Pour 11 tablespoonfuls 'of dilute sulfuric acid into the fifth jar. CAUTION: Do not let any of the acid touch you. Clean the eyedropper and use it to squirt with even pressure the blue solution from the fourth jar into the jar of dilute sulfuric acid. Hold the tip of the dropper under the surface of the sulfuric acid. Finally, remove the result with the glass stirring rod and wash and dry it.

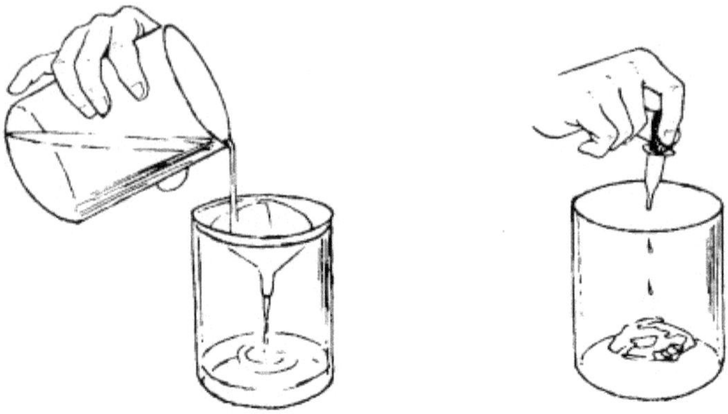

Results: After you added ammonium hydroxide to the jar that contained the filter paper, a thick, dark blue jelly-like substance was formed. This is a cellulose sol. Cellulose is the same substance that makes up the walls of plant cells. It is the basic ingredient of paper and also of all synthetic fabrics. In this experiment, you got cellulose from the filter paper. A sol is a mixture of a liquid and very fine, solid undissolved particles. The solid particles are so densely packed into the liquid that the sol has a jelly-like consistency.

When you squirted the sol into the sulfuric acid, the dark blue became lighter and finally turned white. The sol was changing into a thread of rayon. After washing and drying this thread, it can be used for sewing.

The transformation of the sol into rayon came about through the reaction between the sol and the sulfuric acid. The method you used to make rayon in this experiment is the *cuprammonium* method. Chopped-up wood is the source of cellulose in the commercial application of this method.

HOW TO MAKE YOUR OWN TOOTHPASTE

Gather these materials: Powdered calcium carbonate ($CaCO_3$); powdered orris root; sodium bicarbonate ($NaHCO_3$); essence of peppermint; an empty toothpaste tube; a small bowl; a teaspoon; a pair of heavy-duty scissors; and an eyedropper.

Follow this procedure: Straighten the toothpaste tube. With the scissors, cut off the flat bottom end of it. Rinse the tube out very carefully, including the cap. Replace the cap but pull the other end apart to make a wider opening. Set the tube aside to dry. In the small bowl, mix 2 teaspoonfuls of powdered calcium carbonate and 2 teaspoonfuls of powdered orris root. Add i-teaspoonful of sodium bicarbonate and 3 drops of essence of peppermint. Add water to this mixture, a drop at a time, stirring it constantly until a paste forms. Put the paste into the empty tube by the teaspoonful. Before trying to squeeze the toothpaste from the tube, close the open end by folding it up several times.

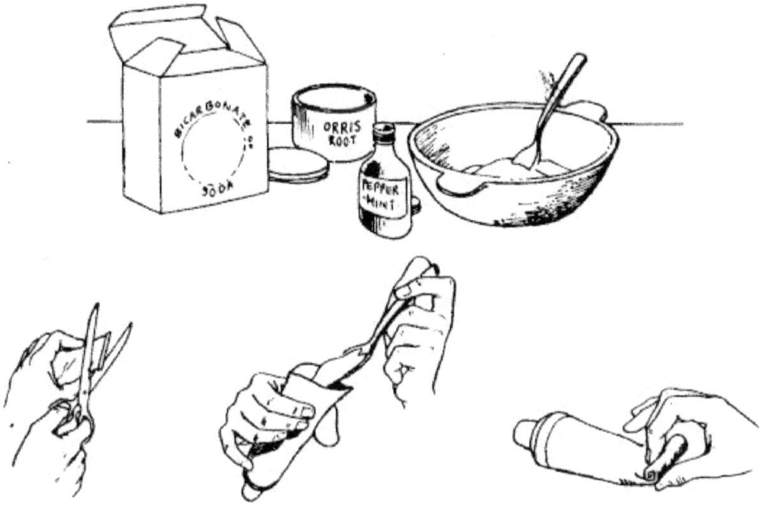

Results: Neither calcium carbonate nor orris root mixed easily with water, but the peppermint and the sodium bicarbonate helped give the paste the right consistency.

You will find your toothpaste inexpensive and pleasant to use. You may have to try making it several times, however, before you learn just the right amount of water to use to get the right consistency.

HOW TO MAKE YOUR OWN VEGETABLE COLORING

Gather these materials: An alcohol burner; ¼ pound of spinach; 1 small beet; grain alcohol; a pot; 3 test tubes; a fork; 2 funnels; filter paper; a glass rod; and 4 glass jars, 3 of them very small. (Get your mother's permission to use the stove.)

Follow this procedure: 1. On the stove, boil the spinach in water for about 2 minutes. Filter the spinach and water through a funnel lined with filter paper into a medium or large jar. Place the spinach and any coloring matter caught in the filter into one of the small glass jars. Add 1 inch of alcohol to it. Put about 2 inches of water in the pot. Then put the glass jar in the pot and heat it on the stove. CAUTION: Keep the flame low because alcohol vapor is flammable. Allow the water in the pot to simmer, but do not allow the alcohol in the jar to get hot enough to boil. Keep stirring and squashing the spinach with a glass rod. After 10 or 15 minutes, strain the spinach, letting the liquid flow into another small jar. Now filter the liquid through a funnel lined with filter paper into a test tube. If the filter paper separates out all or most of the green color, return whatever got caught in the filter paper to the warm alcohol. Repeat the process of heating and filtering. Otherwise, set the funnel aside, and let the liquid stand until the alcohol evaporates from it completely. Then add * test tubful of water to the tube, stir with the glass rod, and pour the contents of the tube into another small jar. Cover it tightly.

Results: The color of your final spinach liquid was green. The green coloring matter in plants is *chlorophyll.* When you boil green vegetables, some of the chlorophyll escapes. In this case, it went into the alcohol, which dissolves chlorophyll. When the alcohol evaporated, what was left was the chlorophyll. The reason for adding water to the chlorophyll afterward is that it is easier to use it as a dye for foods, such as cake icing, in a water solution.

2. Cut the beet into small cubes without peeling it first. Clean the pot and boil the beet in it, in ½ cup of water for ½ hour. Watch it closely, and if the water begins to boil away, add more. At the end of this time, remove the solid pieces of beet with a fork. Pour the remaining liquid through a funnel into a fresh test tube. Try to get a clear solution, but avoid using a filter paper if you can. To do this, let the liquid stand until whatever solid particles are in it settle to the bottom. Allow the filtered solution to stand and evaporate until only ¼ test tube of liquid is left. Transfer the liquid to another small jar and cover it tightly.

Results: The color of the final beet liquid was red. Like chlorophyll, red coloring matter also escapes when you boil red vegetables. It escaped into the water and dissolved in it. After some of the water evaporated, the solution was a little stronger. The red coloring matter in plants and vegetables usually consists of a combination of magnesium and iron salts.

HOW YOU CAN BLEACH COLORED CLOTH BY THE COMMERCIAL PROCESS

Gather these materials: Dilute nitric acid (HNO_3); chloride of lime ($CaOCI_2$); water; 3 small jars; a glass stirring rod; and scraps of discarded colored cotton cloth.

Follow this procedure: Label the three jars A, Band C. Fill all of them t full of plain water. To jar A, add -t of a test tube of dilute nitric acid. To jar B, add t of a test tube of dry chloride of lime. CAUTION: Do not touch either of these chemicals with your hands. If any of the nitric acid or chloride of lime touches your skin, wash it immediately with plenty of water.

Don't put anything in the water in jar C. Stir the contents of jars A and B thoroughly with the glass rod. Now dip a piece of colored cloth into jar A, and swirl it around with the glass rod. Using the same rod, remove the cloth, and holding it above the jar, let it drip for a minute. When most of the excess liquid drains off, transfer the cloth to jar B. Stir again, and again remove the cloth with the glass rod. Transfer the cloth to jar C and rinse it in plain water.

This will remove most of the acid, and you may now safely touch the cloth with your fingers. Hold it under cold running water for a few minutes and then spread it out to dry.

Results: The color disappeared from the cloth. The reaction between the calcium chlorate and nitric acid produced hypochlorous acid (HClO), which in turn caused the bleaching. The equation for this reaction is:

$$2CaOCl_2 + 2HNO_3 \qquad CaCl_2 + Ca(NO_3)_2 + 2HClO$$

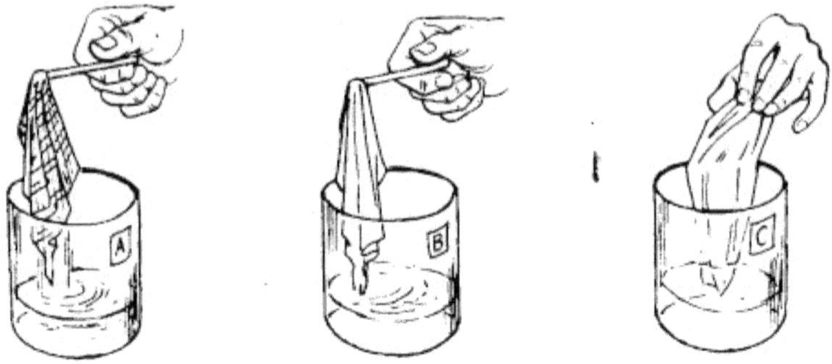

Hypochlorous acid is a chemical from which *nascent* oxygen can be set free. Nascent oxygen is oxygen in its atomic form before it has had time to combine into molecules of O_2. It is a very unstable substance and tries to combine with other atoms or molecules quickly. Here is the equation showing the release of nascent oxygen:

$$HClO \qquad HCl + O$$

Because the nascent oxygen is so quick to combine with other atoms or molecules, it combines almost instantly with the complex dye molecules in the cloth. In doing so, it changes the dyes to colorless compounds. That is why the cloth lost its color.

Most natural fibers, such as cotton and linen, have a yellowish look when they are first manufactured because of the presence of natural impurities. They must be bleached to pure white before they can be dyed, printed, or sold as white fabrics. The commercial process of bleaching these fabrics is very similar to the process you used in this experiment.

The "home" method of bleaching is to use chlorine water, which is chemically similar to hypochlorous acid. Care must be taken when bleaching stains from colored clothes because the dye might be removed as well as the stain. Only cotton, linen, and heavy canvas-type cloth can be bleached successfully with chlorine water.

HOW YOU CAN MAKE SOAP AND DISCOVER HOW IT CLEANS

Gather these materials: Coconut or olive oil; a solution of sodium hydroxide (NaOH); an alcohol burner; a small pot; a tablespoon; a glass stirring rod; a small, amount of kerosene or gasoline; salad or mineral oil; some cigarette lighter fluid; magnesium sulfate ($MgSO_4$); and 8 test tubes.

Follow this procedure: 1. Put 4 tablespoonfuls of coconut or olive oil into the small pot and add 1 test tube of sodium hydroxide solution to it. Carefully heat the liquid over the alcohol burner, using a small flame. Stir the mixture constantly and continue heating it until it becomes a thick paste. CAUTION: Be sure you wear goggles. Sodium hydroxide burns skin and spoils clothing. If any sodium hydroxide gets on your skin, wash it immediately with cool water.

Remember, too, that the pot should never again be used for cooking.

Let the paste cool and rinse it. with water: t.o remove all the excess sodium hydroxide. You may either use this paste as It is or let It dry and become hard.

This "paste" is the soap you will use in the rest of this experiment. If you wish to make a cake of soap also, make some more "paste" and pour it into a small square mold. Then it will dry in the shape of a cake of soap. CAUTION: Use this home-made soap only on your hands. Many people have sensitive skin and such unrefined soap might produce a rash if used on the face or other sensitive parts of the body.

Test Tube No.	*Contents and Treatment of Tube*	*Result*
1.	Water and soap. Shake.	Suds form.
2.	Water and kerosene or gasoline. Shake.	
3.	Water, kerosene or gasoline, and soap. Shake.	
4.	Water and salad or mineral oil. Shake. Let stand.	
5.	Water, salad or mineral oil, and soap. Shake. Let stand.	
6.	Water and lighter fluid. Shake.	
7.	Water, lighter fluid, and soap. Shake.	
8.	Water, magnesium sulfate, and soap. Shake.	

2. Label the test tubes 1 to 8. Then prepare a data sheet similar to the one below

and fill in the information as you perform the rest of the experiment. Follow the procedures as given in the second column of the datasheet.

Results: The combination of water and soap mixed easily with the kerosene, lighter fluid, and magnesium sulfate. The oils, however, did not mix with water or with water and soap together. No matter how hard you shook the mixture, the oils always separated when you allowed the mixture to stand. In other words, the oils did not dissolve in water.

Grease is only another word for oil. It is the grease that makes dust and dirt stick to clothing or skin. Sometimes this grease comes from the normal oils in our skin and sometimes from things we spilled, like gravy or milk. Since grease doesn't dissolve in water, it doesn't do much good to wash dirt with water alone.

Water and soap mixed quite easily, as you saw in this experiment. When you added soap to a mixture of water and oil, something happened to the oil. It no longer separated out from the water. Instead, it broke up into tiny particles that remained suspended in the water without dissolving in it. The water, with the grease particles in it, constitutes an emulsion. As you remember, an emulsion is a liquid containing small, undissolved fatty particles. Soap cleans effectively because it emulsifies grease. Once emulsified, the grease loses its capacity to make the dirt stick. The dirt washes away, therefore, when you rinse the soap away.

If, however, a stain is not merely held by grease, but actually consists of grease, soap will not succeed in washing it away. In that case, you need a grease solvent, such as carbon tetrachloride.

When you added magnesium sulfate to the soap solution, it did not make any suds. Without suds, no cleaning action can take place, because it is actually the suds that do the job of emulsifying the grease. Magnesium sulfate contains magnesium, an element found in many parts of the earth. If magnesium or calcium salts happen to be dissolved in the water people use for washing and drinking, it is called "hard" water. No matter how much soap is added to hard water, no suds form and no satisfactory cleaning can be done. The two minerals that make water hard are magnesium and calcium carbonates and sulfates.

Lightning Source UK Ltd.
Milton Keynes UK
UKHW021853161220
375343UK00008B/375

9 781801 322478